THE BIG
and
Little Five

Dorothy Chang-Van Horn

ISBN: 978-1-66781-657-9

Dedication

*In memory of my mother, Dorothy Chock Chang,
who taught me how to read at age three and
piqued a lifelong yearning for learning.*

*Mahalo to Dad, Dr. Sau Yee Chang, for introducing me
to the excitement and educational value of travel.*

*Shukria to Usha and Mahen Sanghrajka of Big Five
Tours and Expeditions. They fulfilled my dreams
of participating on and escorting safaris.*

*In fond memory of my Chiweenie, Da Chi. She gave
me true love, loyalty, and joy for fourteen years.*

TABLE OF CONTENTS

ON SAFARI IN SOUTH AFRICA FOR THE BIG FIVE AND LITTLE FIVE

For decades hunters sought and shot the dangerous Big Five: Elephant, Cape Buffalo, Rhinoceros, Lion, and Leopard for trophies. These were the five most difficult mammals to hunt on foot. Today, thanks to conservationists, the Big Five are now being shot with cameras by people on safari hoping to bag all Five.

While on safaris in Africa, I'm fortunate to have observed and photographed all the Big Five. The Leopard was the most camera shy.

The Little Five are less obvious than their larger counterparts in South Africa. Few tourists know about these elusive creatures. They include mammals, reptiles, insects, and birds. These smaller beings are namesakes of the dangerous Big Five: Elephant Shrew, Red-billed Buffalo-Weaver, Rhinoceros Beetle, Ant Lion, and Leopard Tortoise. Like the Big Five, these tiny creatures have survival problems due to the impact of climatic changes and humankind destroying their habitat and food source.

Both Fives have fascinating social behavior, means of communication, courtship, mating, parenting, and survival tactics. It's difficult not to attribute humanlike qualities-anthropomorphism while observing their behavior.

The Big Five, especially their courtship and mating behavior, are awesome and amusing. The Little Five's response to their environment cause wonder and delight. Welcome to the fascinating World of the Fives.

CHAPTER 1

GIGANTIC - THE ELEPHANT

Loxodonta africana

On safari in South Africa, my group of five and I are on a quest to view the famous Big Five (Elephant, Cape Buffalo, Rhinoceros, Lion, and Leopard) and less-known Little Five (Elephant Shrew, Red-billed Buffalo Weaver, Rhinoceros Beetle, Ant Lion, and Leopard Tortoise.) We're especially interested to learn whether their courtship, sex life, parenting, and survival have any similarities to we humans.

The morning of our first game drive we are met head on by one of the Big Five, an elephant charging our Land Rover displaying aggressive behavior. The angry bull is agitatedly flapping his ears, threatening us with his raised trunk of 10,000 muscles and vigorously shaking his head. Accompanying this frightening sight is his angry, raucous trumpeting. Our ranger, Patrick, slowly backs his Land Rover away from the furious, gigantic bull elephant charging rapidly at us. He cautions us to remain calm and seated. Any sudden movements, especially hastily accelerating the Land Rover backwards, will further infuriate the charging giant.

It's a great photo op, but the group I'm escorting is paralyzed with fear. James, our spotter, is riding in his bucket seat over the right front bumper. He's ready to shoot the raging bull, hopefully, it won't be necessary.

During my adrenaline rush, I notice strange, dark stuff dribbling from the sides off the bull's head. It looks like the Elephant is crying.

I ask Patrick, "What is that trickling down from his eyes? Is he crying?"

He answers, "Those are not tears. It's secretions from his temporal glands. It's dark and oily secretions called 'musth' because it has a musky smell. It's prevalent when stressed, excited, or searching for a mate. The secretion pours from both sexes while enthusiastically meeting relations. They gallop, run, scream and trumpet excitedly towards each other. Friends and relatives greet each other entwining trunks, placing trunks in each other's mouth, clicking tusks, rumbling, flapping their ears, spinning, and leaning on each other. 'Tears of joy' pour from their temporal glands."

Patrick continues, "Musth appears in bull elephants when they reach sexual maturity between their eighth and fifteenth year. With each year until age forty, the secretions increase copiously. As the bull ages, the flow gradually decreases. During musth, the male elephant is more aggressive and dangerous towards other males and humans. This bull is in musth, that's why he's charging us."

As we are backing away, Patrick tells us to look for the Elephant's temporal glands. "You can't miss them. They're swollen and are between his eyes and ears."

Locating the glands, I imagine smelling musk. As the gigantic member of the Big Five sways towards us, I notice viscous secretions dribbling from his penis and sheath. The dried fluids on his sheath are a moldy greenish white. His hind legs are black with wet patches.

"Patrick, I've never seen elephants with those dark, damp markings. Are they natural?"

Patrick answers "They're caused by he's continuously dribbling urine due to his increased amount of male sex hormone, testosterone. High levels of the hormone stimulate production of innumerable sperm. Increased sperms stimulate him to have numerous copulations. Fertilization is ensured by the large number of sperm in his ejaculation. Male elephants are unique. Their testes are internal, unlike other male mammals. This guy's looking for a mate. Good, he's moving away from us towards that herd of female elephants."

"Patrick, could we follow and watch him? Animal Planet's documentary, "Echo, Queen of the Elephants," showed two huge bulls fighting each other over a female. I've read about elephants courting and having sex but have never seen them."

We move slowly after the giant. Patrick tells us, "Watch him approach that matriarchal herd. His behavior is typical of a male in musth. He's waving his ears to spread his musth scent announcing his presence to females in estrus. His walk is a typical musth walk with head and ears high above his shoulders aggressively warning other bulls away from him. That low pulsating growl, his musth rumble, sounds like a revving diesel engine. Bulls not in musth will avoid him. If there are large bulls that are in musth, you'll see a fight. A strange behavior of a bull in musth is head scratching with a stick."

Photo by Bert Brrr, unsplash

5

Our bull is causing quite a commotion and panic among the matriarchal society of pachyderms. I hear them rumbling a greeting as he gets closer. Like most females, the cows are attracted by his handsome bulk and intoxicating masculine odor. Physically fit, healthy males are preferred instinctively by females. Those fitness characteristics indicate strong genes assuring their young's inheritance of physical fitness and thus their survival. Females attracted to him flirt by reaching their trunks towards him. Others play "hard to get" by turning and backing away from him.

Patrick said, "Watch him. He's searching for a female in estrous (heat). He's noticed that cow in the middle of the herd. She's in estrous, which occurs 2-6 days for four times a year. Puberty for female elephants begins around their 10th or 11th year."

I question him, asking, "How do you know that she's in estrous? She looks no different than the other females."

Patrick replies, "She's surrounded by bulls attracted to her body language. They've probably been chasing and attempting to mate with her. She's rumbling, showing an interest in him. Also, notice the posture of her ears, they are tense. She's in the characteristic estrous posture. She's carrying her head higher than the other females."

As our bull approaches her, the smaller bulls run away from him. A medium-size bull does not flee; ready to compete for mating rights. When our massive bull shoves and tusk pokes him, the would-be competitor runs away.

Patrick comments, "The one that ran is probably not in musth and was frightened off by the larger bull's size and smell. Most females prefer bigger, older, experienced, senior bulls with enormous tusks. This bull is a senior. Senior bulls scare of competitors and do most of the breeding. Females prefer older, hardier males ensuring their offspring's inheritance of traits for survival of the fittest."

Our bull approaches the female. He places the tip of his trunk on her vulva.

Patrick explains the bull's actions. "He's testing her readiness by tasting her urine and secretions from her vulva. By placing his trunk in his mouth, her scent is carried to a specialized gland (Jacobson's organ) on his mouth's roof. If she has a high level of female hormones, scents sent to his brain will tell him that she's in estrous, ovulating, and ready to mate. As you can see, he's testing her frequently. Notice that she's responding to his explorations by urinating, defecating, backing into him, and spinning around. The courtship begins with her walking away from him. He's definitely turned on as he's attempting to catch up with her."

"She looks like she's flirting," I exclaim. "She's looking back over her shoulder while she's walking away from him."

We're instructed to look at her eyes with our binoculars. "She's aware of him," I comment. "Her eyes are not downcast; they're wide open and watchful. It's as if she's giving him a 'come hither' look."

Frustrated with her coyness, I ask Patrick, "If she's interested, why isn't she waiting for him? She's walking several yards away from him with her head and tail raised high. Now she's circling and returning to the herd. Doesn't she want to mate with him?"

Patrick answers, "Her walking and posture is called the 'estrous walk.' It's courtship behavior. He's wants her as you can see from his 'fifth leg' or penis. It is fully erect and touching the ground. Bull Elephant's S-shaped penis is slightly curved and over four inches long to match the female's backward pointing reproductive tract."

Excitedly, I exclaim, "Now he's chasing her and she's running away from him. I'm surprised he doesn't give up and find a willing female."

Patrick comments, "He's interested in her as she probably has a high level of hormones. She's about 10 or 11 years old. If she conceives, she'll be an inexperienced mother. It'll be her first calf. Sadly, if she doesn't know how to nurse her calf, it probably will die. Once he mates with her, he'll stay with her for awhile then look for another cow in estrous. Yeah, the chase can go on for hours and many miles. She can outrun any bull not of her choice."

Finally catching up with her, the bull places his trunk along her neck and head. He rests his long tusk along her rear and pulls himself up over her on his bent hind legs. His front legs are on her pelvis. She's no longer flirting and cooperates by backing into him.

Patrick explains, "He's maneuvering his penis into her downward-pointing vulva. For a successful mating, they must cooperate with each other, or he'll fail to penetrate her. He's already failed several times. His fully erect penis weighs over 60 pounds. It's curving forward and upward as he's searching for the entrance to her vagina. Ah, he's found it and is now in the mounting position as you can see from his straightened hind legs."

Patrick remarks, "That rumbling, groaning, and screaming during their coupling is typical mating behavior. It's referred to as mating pandemonium."

After about a minute, the bull ejaculates. He dismounts and withdraws his penis dripping with semen. Her excited and agitated family runs to her, rumbling, screaming, and trumpeting excited by her loud ultrasonic call (sounds human ears can't detect) during mating. Female relatives touch her mouth and genitals with their trunks.

Patrick says, "Females in estrus create a disturbance and excitement among other elephants. The chasing, copulation, and especially her loud calls, that we can't hear, provoked that pandemonium among her relatives. Sometimes the copulating pair causes the excited herd to urinate, defecate, and back towards the couple. No privacy in their bedroom. Hmm, she hasn't had enough and wants more."

We inquire dubiously, "How do you know that she's ready to mate again? You'd think with all her relatives rumbling and screaming he'd be scared away!"

Patrick replies, "Look, she's turning towards him and reaching her trunk towards his flaccid penis that is still free of its sheath. She's standing parallel to him and rubbing her head against his shoulder. Her long, low, pulsating rumbling, touching him with her trunk, and smelling the sperm on the ground announces that she's ready for an encore. They'll probably stay together the rest of the day and through tonight. He'll follow her and she'll stay close to him. As her consort, he'll chase other courting bulls away from her as long as they are together. By doing so, he protects her from being harassed by them. She won't have to run away from the other bulls' unwanted attention. Thanks to his protectiveness, her estrus is less stressful and exhausting. The couple will stay together while he occasionally mates with her for a few hours during four-days after which she no longer can conceive. When he loses interest in her, he'll leave and look for another female. She'll no longer be protected and be harassed by younger bulls until the aura of estrus disappears. We'll see more elephants during our afternoon drive. It's time for us to return to camp for lunch."

I respond, "We look forward to hearing and seeing more of Africa's largest land animal. Especially interesting will be your explanations about elephant birthing, parenting, and offspring behavior."

During our afternoon drive, James spots a large herd of about 33 elephants. We stop and observe the elephant sorority. Patrick points to three different family units.

I ask, "How do you know that there are three herds and not one large group?"

He says, "Each family unit is following their leader, the oldest and largest female elephant. She's the matriarch of the unit. Watch, that matriarch. When she feeds, the family spreads out and feed. They stay within 50 yards of her. When she stops feeding; they do, likewise, closing ranks, and following her. When she runs away or charges, they follow her lead. If threatened, they cluster around her with calves in the middle. Each family has a matriarch, several of her sisters, her offspring, a couple of her aunts with their families, and her daughters, granddaughters, and young grandsons. Females spend their lives together. The ties between them are very strong. They never quarrel and show each other the greatest tenderness. Typically, each group has 9-11 elephants. These three groups, kinship groups, are related and traveling together."

Patrick tells us about male elephants. "The males have completely different lives than the females. Young bulls are forced leave the group at puberty. Males of the same age are young and inexperienced; they remain close to the females. When they reach the age between 20 and 25, they leave the sub herd they go their separate ways. These bachelors move with great regularity within a well-defined domain, 'bull areas.' Sometimes they have one or two younger males with them. Each male knows his strength from numerous jousts and his place in the pecking order for food, water, water holes, and mating. During the rutting season when they're in musth, they return to the herd. They're ready to find a female in estrous to court and mate. There are several pregnant females in those herds."

We wonder, "How can you tell? They're all enormous!"

"Focus your binoculars between the two front legs of that cow over there," Patrick responds. "Compare her pair of mammary glands, breasts, with the cow to her right. The breasts of the first cow are swollen and her nipples are showing. The other cow's breasts are flat. Swelling and noticeable nipples indicates pregnancy. Her large breasts indicate that she's about ready to give birth. Elephant gestation or length of pregnancy varies, almost two years, around 21-23 months. Although a female can get pregnant a year after a birth, the interval between calves is about 4 to 9 years. Twins are rare. Environmental factors, especially drought, influence pregnancy, the length of gestation, and a calf's survival."

"Have you seen an elephant give birth? How long does it last? A member of my group asks.

"No, I haven't seen a birthing. Viewing one is rare in the wild. If it's her first birth, it'll take about 7 hours. Many births are shorter, especially if the female gave birth previously. Every birth is different; the process is like humans. However, unlike humans, she stands while giving birth and seeks a relative, a midwife, to remain near her and protect her once labor begins. The matriarchal herd is restless during the birthing. They trumpet, snort, and circle around a laboring cow. Her female relatives surround and guard the birthing cow from predators. Dropping her calf, head, and forelegs first, is quick, a few minutes. To prevent attracting predators, mother and relatives quickly remove the after birth. At birth, a calf may weigh and average of 265 pounds for both sexes and occasionally up to 365 pounds for males. A newborn stands about 3 feet tall and is covered with dense body hair. He's born with black or red hair on his forehead, head, and back. After dropping her calf, a mother turns towards the newborn to ascertain that he is alive. She touches him with her trunk and then gently with her forefoot. His mother, sisters, and aunts gather around and assist him to his feet. Once up, they help him find his mother's nipple to suckle his first meal. While sucking with his mouth, his tiny, short trunk dangles to the side. At this early stage, his trunk is used only to search for her nipples. He'll be three or four months before he uses his trunk for other uses. Calves drink about 21 pints of milk, high in fat and protein, per day. Since he's smaller than his gigantic relatives, his mother protects him from being trampled by mistake. He is constantly reassured and comforted by his mother's sniffing and loving strokes. She and the newborn stay on the herd's periphery. They join their family when he's a few days older."

A group member observes, "That baby is so tiny he's having difficulty nursing. I hope he won't starve. What's the survival rate of newborn elephants?"

Patrick answers, "Once they reach puberty, cows are pregnant every four to five years. They birth a single calf during each of those four-to-five-year intervals. About twelve calves are born. One to eight of those births survive."

The astonished group exclaims, "One out of twelve! That's a high mortality rate! Why is it so high?"

Patrick states, "Young calves are easy prey for carnivores and crocodiles. Mothers are vigilant, keeping their babies close to them. Look at that mother over there. That calf is about a year old. He's small enough to walk under his mother, remaining close to her. If he strays 20 yards away, his mother will immediately retrieve him ensuring his safety from lions and hyenas. Although a newborn begins walking within one to two hours, he's shaky and feeble for several days. He's easy prey. I've seen healthy mother elephants become despondent and lethargic for many days after the loss of a calf. Other reasons for the high mortality are droughts causing starvation and dehydration due to lack of water; farmers killing marauding elephants disseminating crops; and poachers slaughtering mothers for their tusks and meat."

Unfortunately, decades of poaching and overhunting of elephants for their tusks has evolved in their being born tuskless. Tusks are teeth-upper incisors. During a baby elephant's first year, his tusks extend from a socket in his skull replacing his milk teeth. Tuskless elephants will be unable to pry bark from trees, dig for water and roots, and as a male, fight other bulls. Hopefully, this calf will develop tusks.

"How long is a calf dependent on his mother?" I inquire. "Also, when is a calf weaned? How does he learn to eat solid food using his milk teeth?"

Patrick answers, "A newborn calf is dependent on his mother for milk and survival.

When there is danger, she pushes him under her. Her relatives surround her for further protection. If it's hot, she protects him from the sun by moving him under her or cooling him by squirting water she's regurgitated from her stomach. I've seen a tender-loving mother boost her young up or down obstacles by wrapping a trunk around his rear and lifting him over a fallen tree or down an embankment. A baby elephant bathing is fun to watch as his mom will place him in a river or water hole, gently squirting him with water, and scrubbing him with her trunk. As a calf grows older, instead of his mother following him, he follows her for protection. Even at 9 years, he wanders no further than a few yards from her. His aunts and sisters also protect and, if lactating, nurse him. Aunts play an important role in childcare. Helping and caring for the youngsters while they grow up is referred to as alloparenting. By alloparenting relatives ensure the next generation's inheritance and survival of their common familial genes. Family bonds among elephants are unbreakable and enduring. The matriarchal herd remains together unless they are separated due to humans and environmental pressure. Mothers and daughters remain together during their lifetime, about 50 years."

Patrick continues answering my question. "Regarding weaning, it varies. During their first year, calves suckle milk several times an hour for about two to three minutes. After that, they suckle once an hour for about two minutes. Weaning may occur as early as their first or second year. Often, calves may nurse 4 years or more until the birth of his sibling.

If his mother dies before he's two, he may also succumb even though his relatives adopt him, providing milk and ensuring his safety. A calf watches his aunts and sisters eating grass, leaves, bark, fruit, and uprooting trees for tender roots with their trunks. Between his fourth and sixth month, his fast-growing trunk enables him to mimic them and sample food. When he is almost three years old, he places his trunk in his mother's mouth to take solid food from it. His diet is a combination of milk and vegetation. Tiny tusks on those youngsters over there will continue to grow in length throughout their lives."

Photo by Dorothy Van Horn

We follow the herd to a waterhole. Patrick tells us that bathing is recreational for young elephants. We watch them as they jostle and climb over each other. Adults join the youngsters in the aquatic gymnastics. We chuckle over elephants of all ages and size gleefully wallowing in mud that's good for their skin. Like straws, their trunks suck up water and then spit it out into their mouths. After drinking, they shower and refresh themselves with water sucked up through their trunks.

Continuing our observation of the matriarchal herd, we watch young elephants playing on the grounds nearby. Young males are rough housing and play fighting. Their trunks are twisting and bodies are whirling. Tiny tusks clash as they attack and spar with each other. Others are dashing back and forth in a floppy, funny gait. Their ears are flapping against their necks and they're holding their curled tails high above their backs. The playtime is accompanied with loud, pulsating, nasal trumpets. Occasionally young adults join in the youngsters frolicking. Their mothers, aunts, and sisters vigilantly watch them. They're constantly on guard protecting them from danger.

Patrick expounds, "The youngsters playing together is essential in learning to interact, practice performing tasks, socializing, and bonding with each other. When they wake up, they immediately play with each other or with a plant or branch. Baby elephants are intensely curious. They're fascinated by birds, tortoises, and baboons. They pretend to charge each other. Proud or frightened by their audacity, they run back and hide behind their mothers. It's believed that romping and playing are essential for development and strengthening of their physiological and anatomical features ensuring survival in their harsh environment. The vigilance among the females indicates a strong bond and cooperation. It's characteristic elephant behavior. Throughout the years, older female relatives will ensure the safety and training of the babies and young adults. Their tender care prepares youngsters for life in a challenging environment. Observe the herd's protective actions. When the family feeds, individuals separate a bit. Now, watch them move towards that hill. They've gathered and bunched tightly together. Indeed, a formidable sight for any hungry predator. The fit and alert will survive and pass their hardy genes on to the next generation."

The unfortunate plight of elephants is emphasized by Patrick. Elephants need to be protected by humans from humans. The pachyderms are threatened by humankind who hunt them for sport, their ivory tusks, meat, and feet for souvenirs. Elephant poaching is ecological sabotage. They shape the landscape by pushing down trees, establishing trails, and creating new areas of grass for other wildlife. They are Africa's Johnny Appleseed dispersing seeds from their dung as they walk through forests and the savanna. Mankind further impacts these gentle beasts by slash and burning the elephants' habitat limiting the animals' grazing area and available water supply. Limited food and water decrease their birth rate and survival of suckling calves. Villagers kill hungry, starving elephants rampaging and destructing their fields. We hope that conservation efforts throughout Africa will successfully improve the future of our world's largest land animal.

We drive and park above a waterhole with bathing hippos. The astonished group watch Patrick and James unfold a table. Its tablecloth is spread with alcoholic and nonalcoholic drinks, chips, carrot and celery sticks, various dips, biltong (Kudu and Impala South African jerky), and spicy meat filled pasties. While enjoying our Sundowner, we watch a mother giraffe and offspring at the waterhole. They spread their long legs and dip their elegant necks towards the water. In the distance we hear the roar of a member of the Big Five, a lion. Our safari's first day ends with a spectacular, flaming, reddish-orange sunset.

Bloat of Hippos   Photo by Dorothy Van Horn

Patrick briefs us regarding our next day's activity. "A staff member will wake you at 4 AM tomorrow morning. A snack of tea, coffee, croissants, and biscuits will be available on the viewing deck. We'll leave from there at 5 AM for our morning game drive. Wear a warm jacket and layer your clothes. Mornings are cold. We need to leave early as the elephant's tiny counterpart, the Elephant Shrew, is most active at sunrise.

Photo by Dorothy Van Horn

CHAPTER 2

TINY - THE ELEPHANT SHREW

Elephantulus myurus

Bleary-eyed, we leave our camp's viewing deck and depart on the Land Rover for the rocky hills. We're huddled under blankets warming us from the cold wind blowing into our open Land Rover. Some of us are unaccustomed to waking so early so we doze on the way. En route we spot a herd of immobile impalas gazing back at us. Patrick chuckles commenting, "They're the savanna's McDonalds. Impalas are easy prey for the big cats, hyenas, and wild dogs."

Impala   Photo by Colin Watts, unsplash

During our drive, Patrick describes the tiny Elephant Shrew and its behavior. We hear that this weird-looking, brownish-grey creature with a mouse-like tail earned his name from his elongated nose. He's distinguished from other shrews by white rings surrounding his brown eyes. Elephant Shrews are most active during sunrise and sunset. His nickname is 'Jumping Shrew.' Because he's elusive, nervous, and shy, we'll be fortunate to see him hopping and jumping around on his territorial, rocky hillside. Elephant Shrews are never seen during the afternoons. They hide from the hot sun in the hill's cool koppies (rocky outcroppings of boulders.) We learn that the creature is misnamed, he is not a shrew. Recent studies indicate that he is a sengi – a term derived from the Bantu language of Africa. He is more closely related to hyraxes, elephants, and sea cows.

Unlike his huge relatives, he's miniscule. The Elephant Shrew is about 10 inches long and weighs only 2 ounces! Small creatures have a short life span. South African Elephant Shrews live about two and a half to four years compared with an elephant's longer life span of at least 50 years.

Elephant Shrew   Photo by unsplash

Patrick discusses the Shrew's outstanding feature, his trunk. "Instead of relying on their excellent vision and hearing, Elephant Shrews explore their habitat with elongated noses. Unlike the herbivorous elephant, he's an insectivore. Like his elephant relative, an Elephant Shrew's trunk-like snout is long and slender with nostrils at its distal end. A trunk enables him to be most successful of all the ground dwelling mammals. His sensitive snout twitches constantly, probing and sniffing every detail of his habitat for food. He seeks and forages for crickets, spiders, termites, ants, and other invertebrates to devour. His long-tapered tongue pushes out to the top of his snout. It continuously darts in and out capturing his prey. His nasal glands' secretions prevent irritation from ants' and termites' chemical defenses. Because of a high metabolic rate, he has a huge daily food intake."

I ask, "Yesterday we saw a strong bond among the elephants. Is the social behavior of the Elephant Shrew similar? If not, how does it differ from his giant relatives?"

Patrick answers, "Elephant Shrews are not highly social like elephants. Like the elephant they secrete a strong scent. Unlike the elephant, the secretion is not from temporal glands but from glands under shrew's tail near its anus. Their scent has many purposes. One of them is for defense. As an Elephant Shrew travels in his territory, he rubs secretions along the ground marking his territory. Unlike other shrews' grassy trails, since the Elephant Shrew's habitat is among rocks, their network of trails is not obvious. They travel from rock to rock with a swift, running gait. Within an hour a shrew marks his territory seven times, each containing an average of 15 glandular secretions. When an Elephant Shrew establishes a new home range, he marks it 5 times during a minute. Studies indicate that their secretions odor is a deterrent against carnivores. Their primary predators are snakes and birds of prey, owls, and hawks. When escaping those predators, his powerful legs run at speeds of over 15.3 miles per hour to their hideout in rocky outcroppings."

I say, "Elephant Shrews don't sound like they're friendly. Do they travel in groups like the elephants?"

Patrick responds," Unlike elephants, Elephant Shrews prefer privacy. Shrews are intolerant of their own species. You're correct. They are not friendly like elephants, nor do they live in groups or with their family. They're not neighborly. If an adjoining neighbor infringes on his territory, crossing his dung barrier, the defender stands on his white feet, high on his powerful hind legs. He slowly walks, mechanically like a robot, up to the intruder. Facing each other, neither one retreats. Their fighting is vicious and rapid accompanied by snapping, loud shrill screeching and screaming. The diminutive 2-ounce pugnacious warriors, like boxers, spar and pummel each other. Their karate kicking is vigorous, rapid, and deadly. Fighters tumble among rocks in a blur of fierce action. The intimidated trespasser is violently evicted and chased out. Fights are between the same sexes. Males defend their territory against invading males. Females defend their habitat fighting uninvited females."

"Do they call to each other like the elephants?" I inquire. "Are Elephant Shrews courtship as intriguing as that of the elephants we saw yesterday? When are they sexually mature?"

Patrick answers, "They vocalize and drum their feet. It's not clear whether vocalization and foot drumming serves a purpose in their social behavior. Some scientists hypothesize that foot drumming occurs when Elephant Shrews are agitated. Other researchers believe that vocalization and foot drumming play a role in courtship. Like bats they communicate with each other by echolocation."

"Remember my mentioning that their secretion has a distinctive odor?" Patrick asks. "Besides marking territory, that odor has several purposes. Shrew's sexes look identical. However, their secretions have different, distinguishing odors. To identify a male from a female, Elephant Shrews smell each other. A male smells like fruit. A female has a sulfurous odor. Every individual shrew has its own unique smell. Elephant Shrews are monogamous. Even though they probably pair for life, they are not affectionate, and are seldom physically together, remaining together only during a female's estrus. They are loners. Despite their standoffishness, a mate readily recognizes the other half of their pair from other couples. Their distinctive odiferous markings enable a pair to distinguish a mate from other shrews, thus maintaining their pair bonding. Even though mates spend little time together, they are surrounded by each other's smell from their continuous markings. Thus, a wife knows and keeps track of her wandering husband and vice-versa."

Photo by Hal Brindley, travel 4 wildlife

Patrick answers my question regarding courtship, "A courting male marks frequently, 5 times during a minute, attempting to attract a female in estrus. Unlike the elaborate elephant courtship, you observed yesterday, Elephant Shrew courtship is brief, thus rarely observed."

We are reminded that Elephant Shrews are monogamous. We're informed that they're among 3% of all mammal species forming such exclusive, monogamous mating pairs.

Female and male Elephant Shrews become sexually mature at 5 to 6 weeks old. Mating occurs in the spring. While courting each other, foot drumming and continuous marking attracts the opposite sex. Courtship and mating occur in the species *myurus* in the spring. Researchers discovered an increase in size of the large and small intestine of both sexes during their courtship and mating. Scientists believe that the enlargement accommodates water absorption during a dry season. The increased size of their gut enables a higher intake of food providing them with much needed energy. That energy is necessary for stimulating a male's courtship and the enlargement of his reproductive organs. In females, extra energy is necessary for lactation and pregnancy. In estrus, a female produces a multiple (over 12 eggs) at each ovulation. Only one or two will develop. Rarely will three eggs develop into embryos. With the increased size of a male's reproductive organs during the breeding season, the frequency of motile sperm also increases. Scientists believe that their breeding season corresponds with seasonal changes from spring to winter influenced by photoperiodism. They noted that a male's digestive tract decreased in size during the winter's wet, non-mating season. Once successfully courted, a female is vigilantly guarded by her mate ensuring monogamy and a lifetime relationship. Both fiercely defend their sex-specific territory from interlopers.

Patrick further informs us that a male is alerted to his consort's estrus period by her increased vaginal marking. Her secretions signal her receptivity. When she's not in estrus, she is agonistic and dominant towards her mate. Such behavior decreases during her brief estrus. Elephant Shrews mate for several days. After mating, the pair separate and return to their preferred solitude within their territory.

Females have litters of one or three born several times a year. Gestation varies from 45 to 60 days. One or two, sometimes three, young are born with each litter. They are large and well developed at birth. Bodies of the newborn are fully furred. They are born with their eyes open. Scientists refer to these birth traits (full development, fur on their bodies and eyes open) as "precocial." Generally, precocial characteristic of animals, such as the Elephant Shrew, distinguish animals who do not build nests for their young from others that do. Unlike newborn elephants, the newly born shrews can run around shortly after birth. However, after being born, they remain in their birthplace for several days.

A mother shrew is not a doting mother. She returns to her nest only to nurse her young. Other than nursing, a mother does not provide direct parental care because their young are precocious. She ignores her young. Her mate is an absentee father.

Offspring are weaned from her teats after five days. Mashed insects are collected and transported in the maternal cheek. The solid food is fed to the young with milk. Slowly the young begin to explore their environment and hunt for insects. After 15 days, the youngsters are no longer dependent on their mother. They migrate from their nests to establish their own territory a few yards away from their nest. Within 41-46 days, they become sexually active and begin searching for a mate.

Sadly, we learn about the Elephant Shrew's predators and threats. Some African tribes prey on shrews for food. The biggest threat faced by the shrew is a limited habitat. Habitat limitation impacts the animal's available source of food. Also, finding a mate in a limited area is more difficult. As a result, the population of shrews is restricted due to their problem of not being able to find a mate, court, breed, and multiple. Without the ability to have off springs to continue their species, the Elephant Shrew could be endangered.

We search in vain, hoping to see an Elephant Shrew scurrying to his hideaway among the rocks. A few in our group comment that they were fortunate to view the Elephant Shrew on Discovery Channel's segment, Mammals, of its *Life* series. The commentator referred to the kangaroo-hopping shrew by its Bantu name, sengi. Unfortunately, we fail to glimpse the elusive tiny creature in its natural habitat of rocks. Instead, we see another Elephant and Elephant Shrew relative, the Rock Hyrax. Several are basking in the morning sun. Others are dashing and running in and out among the rocks.

Returning to camp for breakfast we see members of the Big Five, Cape Buffaloes. Patrick promises, "We'll see them again during our afternoon game drive.

Rock Hyrax   Photo by Jose Halso, unsplash

CHAPTER 3

WANDERER - THE CAPE BUFFALO

Syncerus caffer

During our late afternoon drive, James spots and points to a herd of Cape Buffalo grazing among acacia trees. Patrick startles us by driving slowly into their midst.

A group member exclaims hysterically, "James warned us that Cape Buffalo are short-tempered and unpredictable. They're considered one of the most dangerous animals in Africa. Are we safe?"

Patrick responds, "Those Cape Buffalos are one of the Big Five and are known as 'Black Death' in Africa. Indeed, those large bovids, looking like a cross between an ox and a cow, are savage, dangerous, and cunning. They're responsible for goring and killing over 200 people throughout Africa each year. As James informed you, they are feared for their quick-temper and won't hesitate to use their massive horns to ram and gore if they feel threatened. They're extremely powerful and run at speeds up to 35 miles per hour."

Patrick's instructions are, "You're safe if you don't make any sudden movements. Don't stand up. Remain quiet. Because we're in the midst of a herd of over 100 buffaloes, you won't need your binoculars. Your observations and concentration will be encumbered by fumbling with binoculars. Look for the characteristics and behavior as I describe these unique, powerful, massively built animals."

He continues, "First of all, tourists misidentify them as Southeast Asian Water Buffaloes. The Cape Buffalo is African and because of his unpredictable, dangerous nature has not been domesticated like his peaceful Asian counterpart, the Water Buffalo. Cape Buffaloes are readily identified by their broad heads; wide, bare muzzle; large, round drooping ears fringed with long hair; and massive, heavy horns. Asian Water Buffalo's horns are not as thick, nor do they have a big, thick black boss (shield) that covers their foreheads like Cape Buffalo.

Water Buffalo   Photo by Alex Azbache, unsplash

Look at that lumbering, 1600-pound dark brown tank over there. His huge horns are about 3 feet wide curving upwards like a bow to 5 feet in length. Those horns flatten, widen, and thicken towards their base. Those base forms a protective cover- a boss, shielding the top of his skull. The boss protects him while defending himself and during breeding fights with other males vying for the attention of females. The horns' base thickens in older males. At maturity those two bumps or boss halves join forming a thicker, more protective shield. Aged males are identified by worn horns that have been continuously brushed against the ground, trees, and bushes. The cow over there has thinner and shorter horns that curve more upward than that of a male. She doesn't have a bony flattened boss like he does.

Males are larger, ranging from 935 to 1914 pounds. The female is smaller. The maximum weight for cows is 1267 pounds."

Cape Buffalo   Photo by Dorothy Van Horn

Patrick continues, "I mentioned age. Old bulls and two-year to four-year old males break away from the large groups. They form their own sub herds, bachelor herds. Bachelor herds surround the main herds. Included in the sub herds of bachelor males are high-ranking males and females, old and invalid buffalo. Young males are leery of the dominant bull, staying away from him. They identify him by the thickness of his horns. Adult bulls spar with each other in play, dominance interactions, or actual fights. During these interactions, a bull slowly approaches another. He gauges his rival's strength and prowess. After watching his opponent for a long while, the challenging bull paws the ground and shakes his head to intimidate his adversary. His frightening body language scares the challenging bull to run away. If a rare fight occurs, the approaching bull lowers his horns and waits for the other bull to do the same. The bulls twist their horns from side to side while fighting. Violent blows of their heads are exchanged, occasionally resulting in serious injury or death. When fights do occur, they are over a female they want for mating. If they are playing, the young bulls rub each other faces and bodies during the sparring session."

Patrick says, "More about age. The cantankerous bulls you've heard stories about are old bulls who've wandered off preferring their solitude. Often, they are outcasts, turned away from bachelor herds. Stories about bulls chasing and outrunning hunters who've wounded and angered them are often about a lone bull. He is unpredictable, quick-tempered, and most dangerous of all African wild animals. He's ready to attack and charges without provocation. At the last minute he lowers his massive head and tosses his victim with his lethal horns."

Patrick continues, "Bulls mature during their eighth to ninth year. Females mature at five years of age. At that age they are ready to mate and calf. Their estrus lasts two to three days. Cape Buffalo are polygamous and are seasonal breeders. Courtship, mating, and birthing occur strictly during rainy seasons, around February to March. Birthing occurs during the early rainy season when food is abundant for lactating females. Mating occurs later during the wet season assuring that after 11.5 months of gestation a calf is born during the early peak of a rainy season. Most of the rare fights, as I mentioned earlier, are between bulls interested in courting the same female in estrus (heat.) High levels of testosterone, the male hormone, and causes fierce competition among males during mating season Superior males usually beat the lower ranking bulls during their courtship maneuvers."

Photo by Dorothy Van Horn

Patrick describes the interaction between bulls while vying for an estrus female's attention, "Subordinate bulls seeking to mate are frightened away by the aggressive, top bull's behavior. His displays are fearsome: lowering and heightening of his horns, running around in threatening circles, stiff-legged walking, grunting-growling, spearing the ground and bushes with his horns, angrily digging and tossing dirt, and violently rubbing his neck against the ground. By the time the cow is in full estrous, the triumphant bull is her consort."

Patrick continues his dialogue, "The triumphant, high-ranking bull selects a cow. He stretches low while approaching her. He checks her estrus status by licking her vulva and testing her urine. He grimaces and curls his lip after doing so. His behavior indicates the chosen female is approaching estrus and is being courted. Prompted by his approach and licking, the cow responds by urinating. If she's not interested, she moves away. Her evasiveness attracts the attention of many bulls. She's being selective, searching for inheritable strong traits such as muscular bulk and massive horns, assuring a better survival rate for her offspring. If she shows an interest in the dominant bull's advance, he responds by staying near her, protecting her from the advances of other bulls. This bonding is not always appreciated by the evasive cow whose wandering eyes continue looking at other bulls approaching her. Courtship behavior continues for several days. When a bull's advances finally are accepted, the cow submits by standing still with her tail arched and pushing her muzzle under his belly. He responds to her readiness by resting his chin on her rump. When she complies and doesn't bolt, his forelegs clasp her around her pelvis. He mounts the receptive cow. Copulation is a minimum of two times within half an hour. The sight of the copulating pair excites other bulls who gather around and fight among themselves. Cows in heat have been seen mounting and humping other cows. Flirting females have been observed initiating mating by placing chins on a male's rump and/or urgently muzzling him under his belly."

I inquire, "Do Cape Buffaloes have multiple births like Elephant Shrews or are they more like Elephants giving birth to one calf? What's the weight of a newborn?"

Patrick answers, "Eleven and a half months after mating, a single calf is born. Twins are rare. A calf weighs almost 90 pounds. The calf is dropped amid the herd. Within 10 minutes of birth, calves have been known to rise on wobbly feet from their birthplace. Buffalo calves are too feeble to follow and keep up with the herd. A newborn is poorly coordinated and a very slow runner. In such a weakened state, newborns are easy prey for lions, wild dogs, and hyenas. Unlike elephants, the buffalo herd does not remain with the mother and her calf. They move away to graze and drink. They abandon the mother to fend for herself and calf. She attempts to protect her young by leading him into the nearest cover and hiding him until he's strong enough to follow her back to the herd. Or she may attempt to remain with her herd by urging him to follow her by croaking at him. She shuttles indecisively between her herd and calf. She's torn between her desire to remain with her group and her desire to follow her maternal instincts. Sometimes the urge to return to and remain with her herd is stronger than her maternal instincts. She abandons her young calf. Without her protection, he's easy prey for lions, wild dogs, and hyenas. If there is a strong bond between mother and calf, they remain together longer than cattle. Mothers who bond with their calves have sons remaining with her for up to two to four years before they join a bachelor herd. Like elephants, daughters remain with their mothers much longer, sometimes a lifetime. Calves are kept within the herd's center for protection."

Patrick continues, "You're probably curious about buffalo nursing. Buffalo like cattle have teats, not nipples like elephants. Unlike cattle's calves, buffalo calves nurse between their mother's hind legs. A buffalo calf suckles for 3-10 minutes at a time during irregular intervals. Suckling occurs until his sibling is born. A female buffalo stops lactating during her seventh month of a second pregnancy that occurs around her first calf's 10th or 15th month. Since milk is no longer available, he is weaned. Her teats are his pacifiers. The interval between births ranges from 15 months, under good environmental conditions, to two years. With the birth of a new calf, the yearling's mother chases him away by jabbing him with her horns. In spite of her unloving prods, the yearling follows his mother for another year or longer. Like elephants, males between the age of one or two leave their mothers. They regroup with other young males forming a bachelor herd. Young females remain with the herd."

We watch calves and yearlings at play and bonding with each other. They are running and chasing each other with tails arched. Like the elephants we observed yesterday, the young are sparring among themselves. The sparring is for play rather than dominance or actual fighting. Calves learn to interact and socialize with each other during these playful bouts. Their elders watch them protectively and do not join in the youngster's antics.

We're told that when chased by their major predator, lions, a herd will remain close together. By doing so, it makes it difficult for the predator to pick off one of its members. Calves are gathered in the middle of the herd. A stray calf sends a call of distress when he is stalked by a lion. He cries in the same croaking call given by his mother when she's looking for him when he lags. His distress call triggers his mother and the herd's attention. They respond in a mobbing behavior. His mother and herd charge and chase the lion. They may tree him and keep him treed for hours. Lions, out run by a maddened herd, have been trampled by buffaloes of both sexes. When a member is caught by a predator, the herd rushes to and rescues the victim by goring and tramping on his captor. It takes multiple lions to bring down, kill, and eat a single adult Cape Buffalo bull. Only large, solo male lions are known to take down an adult buffalo. Old solitary buffalo and young calves are easy prey for the Nile Crocodile. A newborn calf is easy prey for the leopard, lion, and spotted hyena.

We're told that Cape Buffalo are wanderers. They move about, grazing in a variety of habitats. They range on open plains through savannah woodlands, such as the one we're occupying, to river's edge. Buffalo prefer dense cover such as reeds and thickets for protection and shade. African Buffalo are nonterritorial, gregarious, extremely sociable, and protective of each other and their territory. A herd may have up to 1600 or more bovids. They're one of the most successful African mammals, over a million throughout the continent, with a vast geographical range.

Photo by unsplash

Cape Buffalo need grass, shade, and a plentiful source of water drunk twice daily. Cape Buffalo are vegetarians. They're referred to as "bulk grazers" because they feed on large quantities of low-quality food. As vegetarians they subsist on grasses too tall and coarse for other grazers such as Antelope and Wildebeest. Unlike most grazers, they are less partial to young tender shoots. Their massive cheek teeth, broad row of incisors and adept prehensile tongues enable them to quickly gather and bundle long grass. They feed from 5 to 10.5 hours throughout the day and night. Buffalo efficiently consume more grass than other grazers. Cape Buffalo play an important ecological role by reducing the height of tall grasses exposing shorter, higher-quality grasses that are favored by pickier and selective feeders-Gazelles, Reedbuck, and Impala.

Someone notes, "They're several red and yellow-billed birds perched on buffalo backs. A couple pecking in his ears. The buffalo don't seem to mind having those hitchhikers on them."

Photo by Lewie Embling, unsplash

"Those are Red and Yellow Bill Oxpeckers." Patrick informs us. "Oxpeckers with yellow bills pluck parasites. The Red Bills use quick sideways scissoring movements through the buffalo's hair. Both species are searching for and devouring ticks. They cling to their hosts with sharply curved, pointed claws. They're stiff and pointed tails prop them against their hosts. Those two Oxpeckers in that buffalo's ears spend lots of time working deep in his ears. They sometimes work so deeply and intensively that only their tail shows. They also forage for parasites around the muzzle, eyes or nose of their tolerant host. Oxpeckers spend most of their lives on their hosts. They use the hosts for protection from predators (such as moving to the back side of their host when approached) and sitting on them to roost and preen. The mutualism benefits both the host and birds. The birds benefit from their feeding and host's protection. The host benefits by being rid of parasites and warned by the Oxpeckers' screeching and flying away warning him of approaching danger."

Patrick says as he points to a group, "Look at those resting bovids clustered closely together. They are typical of Cape Buffalo's social behavior. Members of the same clan lie together with backs touching or their chin supported on a companion's back. Their need for close contact and being near each other is a distinguishing characteristic of Cape Buffalo.

Unlike the dominant matriarch led herds of elephant, buffalo herds have a pecking order. Linear dominance is clearly defined and jealously maintained by threatening displays and fighting. Dominance by pecking order is maintained within the separate sexes: males dominate males and females dominate females. At the top of this hierarchy, an adult male dominates over females and other males."

Patrick informs us that if we were viewing Cape Buffaloes near a water or mud hole, a dominant male would be readily identified by being sole proprietor of the hole. Dominant males wallow most frequently, spending a couple of hours a day in mud holes, especially during hot afternoons. Dominant bulls are further identified by their aggressive actions of digging and tossing mud with their horn, kneeling, neck- rubbing, rolling and urinating. Subordinate bulls quickly leave a mud hole to superior males.

At the conclusion of a successful game drive, we stop for another relaxing Sundowner on top of a hill overlooking a savanna of grazing zebra and feasting wildebeest. Our group excitedly exchange features observed during its exhilarating, unexpected close encounter with one of nature's nastiest creatures-- the African Buffalo.

Photo by unsplash

Patrick briefs us regarding our next day's activities. "We'll be on an afternoon game drive and a morning walking safari. During our walk we'll be looking for the four remaining members of the Little Five. Include water in your back or fanny packs. As you did for our early morning drive, layer your clothes with a jacket on top. You'll be peeling off each layer as the day's temperature progresses from cold to hot."

My group is especially interested in finding the Cape Buffalo's counterpart, the Red-billed Buffalo Weaver. Hopefully we'll be more successful than this morning's attempt to find the wily Elephant Shrew who eluded us.

CHAPTER 4

SETTLER - THE RED-BILLED BUFFALO WEAVER

Bubalornis niger

After breakfasting our group meets Patrick and James for our first walking safari. Patrick gives us strict instructions, "You're to follow me in a single file. James will be the rear guard. No loud talking, please. I'll point at what I've spotted. When I raise my hand, stop, and gather around me. If we are near Rhinos, Cape Buffalo, and the large cats, Leopards and Lions, - do NOT run! Freeze and no sudden movements! Be a tree! By remaining quiet and still, you won't attract their attention. They'll ignore us and continue on their way."

Intimidated and cautious, our group follows Patrick as instructed. Both he and James are carrying rifles. Hopefully, it won't be necessary for them to fire their guns."

We're not far from our camp when we hear a mellow trilling. Patrick signals us to stop near a large, tall, bushy Flat-Crown Acacia tree. There we observe flocks of small, black, and dark brown birds flitting, perching, and flying among the tree's branches and on the ground.

Hurrah! We found one of the Little Five, the Red-billed Buffalo Weaver. Compared to its larger counterpart, the Cape Buffalo, the bird is diminutive. It measures about 9 inches and weighs less than 3 ounces. These weavers resemble and are slightly larger than sparrows. Like its massive counterpart the Cape Buffalo, Red-billed Buffalo Weavers are gregarious and social. Weavers are the second largest bird assemblage throughout Africa. These birds are extremely noisy and active. The mellow trilling that attracted us is followed by noisy, loud, falsetto croaking and raucous chattering.

Photo by Hal Brindley travel 4 wildlife

Patrick comments about the weavers' calls. "You're hearing a wide range of different vocalizations. Those sounds you hear are not regarded as songs such as those you've heard songbirds warbling. Certain sounds that Buffalo Weavers emit advertise and warn intruders away from their territory. Those warning sounds are harsh and repetitive chatter. If you listen carefully, you'll note that these birds' sounds are not tuneful. They aren't producing musical notes. Their courtship calls attract birds ready to mate."

Patrick compares the female weavers with the males. The females, like most birds are plainer than their opposite sex. Females are dark brown with variable flecks of white on their underparts. Their appearance is mottled. The female's bill and legs are brown. The males are black, black, black, black---black heads, black throats, black legs, and black backs. Emphasizing and contrasting the male's stark blackness are orange eyes, red legs, and red bills. There are two species of Buffalo Weavers deriving their names from the color of their bills. White-billed Buffalo Weavers have very thick, conical white bills. The Red-billed Buffalo Weavers have rounded conical red bills. You're looking at Red-billed Buffalo Weavers. When they are in flight, you'll see flashes of white patches on their black wings. We readily distinguish the dowdy mottled, brown females from the larger, sooty black males. When the males ruffled their black plumage, we saw the white base of their feathers flashing at us.

Photo by Hal Brindley, travel 4 wildlife

"They're about 50 birds in this colony," remarks Patrick. They're noisy because branches of this tree is where they are nesting and defending their nest. Weavers are aggressive defenders against predators and other members of their own species, driving them off with loud threats and fierce body language. There are one or more males who are the principal defenders. They recognize their nest-family members and protect them and their nests from strangers of the same species. If the defending males are away from the nest, a female takes over the defense tactics."

While we watch the raucous, foraging birds on the ground and at the big tree's base, Patrick says, "Their rounded and conical bills are adapted for devouring their primary food – seeds. Besides searching for seeds, they're also looking for fruits and ants. Those flying above us are hawking and swooping for butterflies, bees, wasps, and locusts. Buffalo Weavers attack their flying prey aerially and feed while flying. They also may take their prey to a secluded place where they kill the prey, tear it into small bits, and devour the small pieces."

Patrick points at the fork of branches towards the top of the tree. Among the branches are weavers that have joined forces in building a home. They're flitting in and out among the branches, noisily and busily weaving coarse grasses with untidy twigs into messy nests. There's no obvious pre-planning in their frantic efforts.

Patrick comments, "Weavers build nests in large, isolated trees such as this Acacia. Those males are building a communal nest. Weavers do not apply adhesive to hold their unruly nest together. Functional resistance holds that mixture of coarse grass and bulky twigs together. Their messy, shared nests may reach up to 10 feet and 15 feet in width. Such a huge nest may hold up to three hundred pairs of breeding weavers."

We're told that unlike other weaver species, such as the bright, golden Cape Weavers, Buffalo Weavers are unimaginative architects, sloppy build-ers, and untidy housekeepers. Their bulky, bedraggled nests' have thirteen or many more inner chambers. Chambers have side entrances woven into vertical tunnels facing upwards. The tunnels gradually widen into the nest's chambers.

"Unlike Cape Weavers where each monogamous pairs builds and lives in one neat, tidy nest of their own, the Buffalo Weavers live in groups. They are colonial. They settle in apartments, not in separate nests like the Cape Weavers. Communal males invite and entice females to mate with them after constructing their irregularly shaped nest.

Successfully paired, noisy couples busily flit in and out selecting an apartment where they settle and begin housekeeping. The male lines the couple's chambers with green vegetation. Later a fertilized female will add more lining to the chamber before laying her eggs. Mating does not occur in the nest. Mating pairs fly to neighboring trees. Their mating is a noisy, demonstrative affair." Patrick informs us.

Photo by Dorothy Van Horn

We're overwhelmed by Patrick's descriptions of the Red-billed Buffalo Weavers eclectic, varied sex life. Mating occurs during the dry months, mainly October through April.

Unlike most birds, Buffalo Weavers are bigamous. Communities with several mating pairs have a dominant male mating with as many females as possible. Colonial weavers are polygamous with one dominant male and several breeding females. In the weaver's polygamous system, a male rules and defends up to eight chambers in the large communal nest. Each of the ruling male's chambers houses a female and a young.

Red-billed Buffalo Weavers are also polygamous with one dominant female mating with several males. Scientists studying the genetic make-up of young Buffalo Weavers noted multiple paternities among the brood.

Sexually the male, Red-billed Buffalo Weaver is unique. Male weavers are unique because most bird couples breed by pushing their rear ends together in a "cloacal kiss" whereby spermatic fluid is rubbed against the female. A male Buffalo Weaver "kisses" and has a unique appendage to arouse himself and his chosen mate. The male Buffalo Weavers are more like male mammals than most male birds. Incredibly Buffalo Weavers have a false phallus – penis. Unlike mammalian penises his does not have blood vessels or spaces (corpus cavernosum) to accommodate engorged blood vessels during erection. Due to the lack of blood vessels, an aroused male weaver does not have an erection.

A Buffalo Weaver's penis is used to stimulate his mate while breeding. His penis is .6 inches with a twisted furrow through its length. Males in communal nests have lengthier penises than males living alone. Once again, size is a factor in the social success of animals. Females select males with longer penises. By doing so, they're selecting mates with stronger traits. This ensures their offspring will inherit genes resulting in a better chance for their young to survive and continue their species.

Patrick tells us about behavioral ecologist Tim Birkhead's studies and observations of the Red-billed Buffalo Weaver. Birkhead published his studies of the Buffalo Weavers' remarkable false phallus in *Nature*. In his document, he mentioned seeing and noting Buffalo Weavers' eight matings during a period of three years.

Birkhead reports observing a couple living communally in a large stick nest. "A frisky pair would occasionally emerge and fly to a nearby tree. There the amorous pair would bounce numerous times up and down on top of each other. They'd be at each other for 10-20 minutes. Compared to the 1-2 second cloacal kisses of most birds, Buffalo Weavers' staying power is unique."

Patrick informs us that other studies indicate that a male does not insert his penis for copulation with a female. The penis is used adeptly during foreplay. By rubbing his penis against a female, the stimulated, excited male increases his sperm production. The increased production ensures a successful mating and improves chances of fertilizing his mate's eggs. Amazingly, by massaging his penis against her during foreplay, he reaches climax and orgasm.

According to Birkhead's report, at climax the Buffalo Weaver males' eyes glaze over. Males shake and shudder during an orgasm. A first in the world of birds!

After mating, the satisfied male departs leaving his mate to fend for herself. She flies to their apartment in the communal nest. She busily prepares it for her eggs by adding lining to her nest.

Photo by Dorothy Van Horn

During spring and summer, a Buffalo Weaver female lays three to four fertilized eggs. Without help from any of the males with whom she mated; she incubates her eggs for 11 days. Eggs hatch between 20-23 days. The hatchlings are naked, blind, and helpless. They need more parental care than birds that are hatched with their plumage. When they feather, the fledglings resemble mottled dark brown adult females. Males do not usually acquire breeding, black plumage until at least their second year. The mother is a single parent. She fends for her young and feeds them seeds until they are ready to fly from their nest.

Red-billed Buffalo Weavers are successful survivors. They are not threatened by humans or known predators. They will continue to survive provided their habitat of large trees is not destroyed by an increasing presence of humans.

We leave the frantic, noisy birds and continue our walking safari. During our walk Patrick identifies a variety of trees, among them Bushman's Tea and the famous upside-down Baobab. The wild flowering plants are colorful, especially the Wild Garlic, Guinea Fowl Aloe, and Spider Flower.

Patrick points at animal and bird footprints and their droppings. We see footprints of a lion, one of the Big Five. On the sandy road, we watch a Dung Beetle rolling the poop of another Big Five, an elephant.

We walk onto the flat sand away from the road. We're on sandy soil that is pock-marked with several holes. Patrick stops us to look at the tiny craters. We're told that they are pit traps dug by one of the Little Five, the larvae of Ant Lions. He pointed at their jaws poking out from their hiding places.

If James had not shown us a green chameleon camouflaged on a shrub's brown branch, we would not have noticed it. We observe it change colors, from brown to green, as it moved from the branch to the shrub's green leaves.

Photo by unsplash

We stop at another bush. James plucks a large leaf from it. We're told that natives, the Xhosa, use leaves from the bush for toilet paper. Later he plucked a twig from another bush. Stripping and shredding its tip, he demonstrated its use as a toothbrush. Native survival in the bush!

Returning to camp Patrick points at a huge beetle. "Because of the horns on its head, it's called the Rhinoceros Beetle. It's one of the Little Five. We'll be searching for its larger counterpart, the Rhinoceros, after lunch during this afternoon's drive.

CHAPTER 5

WIDE-LIP: THE WHITE RHINO

Ceratotherium simum

AND

POINTED-LIP: THE BLACK RHINO

Diceros bicornis

During our afternoon drive, James spots a grazing White Rhino with her calf. Patrick expounds about these ungainly animals resembling the now extinct Triceratops. He says the name "rhinoceros" comes from ancient Greek meaning, "horned nose. "Like its prehistoric ancestor, the Rhino is in danger of extinction due to global climate changes impacting its environment and man's lucrative poaching. There are only 5 species of Rhino left making them one of the most critically endangered species.

Rhinos are diurnal, most active during the day. Rhinos are loners. They are creatures of habit, using the same trails daily and following precise schedules. They're tolerant of other animals grazing and browsing in their territory. They share waterholes with them. However, they do not tolerate intrusive Rhinos. Outsiders are systematically chased out of the resident Rhino's habitat.

We're told that the White Rhino is the second largest land animal (although outweighed by the hippopotamus) after elephants. Like the elephant, they are gentle giants. The slate gray, White Rhino is larger than the dark gray Black Rhino. The White Rhino is gregarious and tolerant of other White Rhinos and tourists. It is placid and the most sociable of the two. are grazers in open spaces, unlike the solitary Black Rhino, browsing among trees. Female White Rhinos feed close together in groups of 10 or more. Like both sexes of the Black Rhino, White Rhino males are loners. The urge of both male species to mate with an estrus female takes them temporarily out of their bachelorhood.

White Rhino   Photo by Dorothy Van Horn

Black Rhino   Photo by unsplash

The two Rhinos differ in temperament. The Black is short-tempered. Both sexes of the Black are easily offended. Blacks have a reputation for unprovoked aggression. They are easily aroused, unlike their placid sociable White Rhino cousin. Rhinos are poached for their horns. The horns are valuable. They are sold in Southeast Asia and the Middle East (for medicine, aphrodisiacs, and dagger handles). Prized by Middle Easterners and Southeast Asians, the Rhino horns are not like antelope horns. Rhinoceros horns are like our human hair and nails containing keratin. Their horns contain no bone. The two tandem horns consist of a tight hard mass of tubular filaments, outgrowths of the skin which is not attached to the bone of their skull. The larger, light gray, White Rhino's front horn's maximum length is about 59 inches. It's larger than the rear horn. The smaller, darker gray Black Rhino's fore horn measures about 41 inches. The two horns are more equal in size than those of his relative, the White Rhino. Both species have very poor vision and depend on their excellent sense of hearing and scent to run from danger. The two are readily distinguished from each other when they are running or trotting away from opponents or danger. The White Rhino holds his head near to the ground. The Black Rhino runs or trots with his head held high.

Black Rhinos are on the brink of extinction. Black Rhinos are territorial and are, therefore, easily spotted and killed by poachers and shot for trophies by hunters. White Rhinos, although endangered, are more fortunate because of their extensive home range. They outnumber the Black by several thousand due to effective protection, conservation, and management in South Africa.

We stop to observe and learn about the grazing White Rhino and her calf. This Rhino's name is explained to us. When the Dutch settlers saw this massive species with its wide, square mouth, they described it in Dutch: "'Wyd or wide." Misinterpreted, the word evolved to White. More correctly, the White Rhino should be referred to as "Square-lipped Rhinoceros."

Surprisingly, neither species have incisors or canines. Their lips are used for grazing or browsing. The White Rhino has a square upper lip for grazing on grass. It is exclusively herbivorous, grazing with its muzzle (like must ruminants) continuously against the ground. They crop the grass very closely to the ground giving their grazing area a lawn-like appearance. The White Rhino's favorite habitat is grassy woodland, with short grass and plenty of water. Trees in the woodland provide necessary shade protecting White Rhinos from the hot African sun.

Black Rhinos have a pointed, prehensile upper lip for browsing. They should be referred to as "Hook-lipped Rhinoceros." A prehensile hook-shaped upper lip enables them to easily strip leaves of trees, twigs, soft branches, and shrubs. Trees are pushed over to better reach food. Shoots of plants are guided into their mouths with prehensile upper lips. Shoots are bitten off by pre-molars and ground up between massive molars. Black Rhinos are selective diners. They prefer milky succulents, leaves of acacia and euphorbia, and most of all the sausage tree's woody fruit. Black Rhinos seek well-developed woodlands or thickets for both food and resting. They are more dependent on water than the White Rhinos. Black Rhinos are very vulnerable to severe drought because of their territorial and sedentary nature.

Continuing to watch the White Rhino mother and her calf, we notice the calf following its mother. Patrick informs us that another method for identifying the White from the Black species is whether a calf is in front of or back of his mother. "When the White Rhino and her calf leave an area on the flat savanna, she pushes her calf ahead of her. On the open plain, chased animals are attacked from the rear. The White Rhino can best protect her young by covering his vulnerable rear. The Black Rhino mother is the path finder; she leads and clears the way for her calf through thick bush."

Like Cape Buffalo, both Black and White Rhinos breed and birth throughout the year. In South Africa, the White Rhino's mating season peaks during the rainy season, October to December. After a 16-month gestation, they give birth to a single calf during the late rainy months. Global warming is impacting the breeding and birthing of the Rhinos, as it is for all African mammals. Drought results in a domino effect: no food causes insufficient lactation by nursing mothers, starvation of mother and calf, dehydration from lack of water and eventually death of the weakened animals. The less fit is easy prey for the big cats, hyenas, and wild dogs.

Female White Rhinos mature at 6 to 7 years. Their estrus cycle occurs at monthly intervals. Males mature at 10 to 12 years. Black Rhinos reach puberty a year younger than that of the White Rhinos, 4 to 6 years for females and 7 to 9 years for males.

Patrick relates the difficulties of courtship among the White Rhinos. "It's a risky process for a bull attempting to wear down a female's resistance to his courting overtures. He vocalizes his interest by serenading her with hic-throbbing, his version of a love song. The smitten suitor follows his chosen mate, rests his heavy chin on her rump, and attempts to mount her. She responds to his hic-throbbing serenade with mouthing-chewing movements and threat displays. If not interested, she mock or real attacks him with threatening snarls. The cow constantly evades and avoids contact with him prolonging his advances from 5 to 20 days. She responds to his approaches by frequently urine-spraying. Amazingly, the smitten bull shows remarkable restraint, especially during her urine displays. Instead of chasing and blocking her squealing attempts to escape, he keeps the distance, 60-98 feet, she sets until she comes into full estrus. Keeping within his safety zone, he wails loudly communicating that he doesn't want her to leave him. When she allows him near her, like Cape Buffalo males, he tests and tastes her urine for levels of estrogen. He grimaces raising his upper lip stimulated by sex hormones present in her urine. The smitten bull croons his love song and cautiously continues approaching his elusive love. Wisely, he retreats when she threatens him or when his advances are prevented by her calf or juvenile companion. After many days of his courtship, she finally yields to his patient persistence by allowing him near her. Triumphantly, he nudges her with a horn and his head. He lovingly muzzles her sides and shoulders. Then he rests his massive chin on her huge rump. He preliminary mounts her. At last, after his enduring preliminary efforts of 15-20 hours, she stands still with her tail curled. The bull places his forelegs around her hips and mounts her. He successfully copulates with her for half an hour."

Patrick remarks, "Rhinoceros, like Lions, are sexually powerful. Rhinos mating can last up to an hour with several ejaculations. Erect, the penis of a Rhino male is over three feet. Because of their sexual prowess, Rhinos are hunted for their horns by poachers. Southeast Asians, especially the Chinese, will pay exorbitant prices for Rhino horns that are ground into powder for an aphrodisiac, Asian Viagra. The Asians believe, erroneously, that they will have sexual stamina like the Rhinos." They also believe the powder cures all sorts of ailments such as coughs, fever, pain of childbirth, measles, etc. Further decimating the entire continent of Africa's rhino population is Yemen's demand for the rhino's horns. In the past three decades nearly 54,000 pounds of horns have been illegally exported to Yemen. More than 22,000 rhinos have been killed since 1970 to meet the demand. The horns, each worth $1 million, are used to make the Jambiya dagger's handle. The dagger is traditionally carried by Yemeni men representing their male honor, wealth, and strength.

Patrick continues informing us about Rhino mating behavior. "The pair of Rhinos you see mating will remain together up to five days. During that period, copulation is not as frequent. Sometimes estrus females consorting with their mate form feminine pair bonds. When their male partner is not with them and another male appears seeking to mate, he is chased away by one of the consort's loyal females. The returning consort is welcomed by his faithful females who willingly succumb to his mating overtures."

We're awed by the White Rhino bull's persistence and his consort's loyalty. One of us asks, "Is the Black Rhino courtship identical with that of the White? Since Black Rhinos are more aggressive than White Rhinos, is a Black Rhinoceros as patient or does he demand immediate gratification?"

Patrick chuckles answering, "A meeting between a Black Rhino bull and cow is characterized by a lot of bluff and bluster. It's marked with puffing snorts by either or both. A bull approaches his chosen female cautiously. His body language displays his interest in her. His head is lowered and ears forward. He thrashes his head from side to side or roots the air with his horns. He's bluffing, testing her response to his advances. If she turns or lunges at him, he wheels and gallops away. Undaunted, he returns and circles around her. She squeals at him and turns away. He continues cautiously approaching her by rushing, jabbing, horn-clubbing, puffing, and dunging. She responds by frequent spray-urination, chewing side-to-side, squealing with threats, and mock or real attacks warding off his unwanted advances. Their performance continues for more than two hours. If the female is approaching her estrus, his enduring advances finally result in her yielding to his overtures. A tender, loving bond forms between the two."

Patrick continues describing the Black Rhino's mating. "The successful suitor grimaces while tasting and testing her urine for levels of estrogen. He then begins the time-consuming task of conditioning her to accept contact with him. He begins a series of preliminary mounts without erection. During her full estrus, his series of attempts goes on for hours interspersed with periods of feeding and walking. Finally, the pair copulates for half an hour during which the cow stands quietly, emitting a low-pitched squeal and mouthing expressions (chewing vigorously side to side.) During her 3-day estrus, a female may mate with several vigorous bulls."

I comment, "Wow! The Black Rhino is more demonstrative, aggressive, and persistent than the White Rhino! And, unlike the White Rhino she consorts with more than one bull."

Patrick laughingly says, "I left out the unromantic overtures of the courting Black Rhino.

Besides groaning, charging, head and horn butting and pawing the ground, he defecates and sprays urine!"

"No wonder the female he's courting continuously rebuffs his advances! She probably finally yields to his advances not because of his enamored crooning but more from seeking relief from his odoriferous approaches," I exclaim. I change the subject from gross mating behavior to that of parenting. "Do the two species differ in their parenting behavior? How are they similar?"

Patrick answers, "When ready to calve, the White Rhino seeks dense cover. She remains secluded several weeks before returning with her newborn to her home range and routine. Within an hour after his birth, her newborn stands unsteadily for a couple of days. During his wobbly state, his mother successfully fends off predators. Her newborn weighs 143 pounds, equal to 4% of her weight. She responds to his hungry whining and begging by nursing him for two to three minutes or until he's satisfied. She is relieved from his constant demands by his beginning to graze when he is two months old. He is weaned when he is a year old. A White Rhino calf and his mother have an enduring bond. Calves remain with their mothers for about five years."

Patrick continues responding to my question. "Regarding the expectant Black Rhino cow, like her relative she seeks isolation. She drives her previous offspring away from her seclusion. Her rejects are still too young to fend for themselves. Although cows with calves are generally solitary, they occasionally take in subadult females and males rejected by their mothers. They protect and ensure the survival of the rejects. Like their White Rhino cousins, the Black Rhino newborns can stand within 10 minutes. Nursing is like that of the White Rhino. For protection, calves follow closely to their mothers. A calf who loses sight of his mother will pant in a contact call. When threatened, a young calf failing to call out for help is easy prey to hyenas and lions. In spite of her bulk, an enraged White or Black Rhino mother can turn on its own length and at a full gallop of 40 mph rescue her imperiled calf. Hearing the calf's squeaking, his mother's companions rush to her aid. A newborn with an inexperienced, young mother responding too slowly is easy and helpless prey. When alarmed, a White Rhino's calf gallops ahead of his mother. A Black Rhino speedily follows his mother as she crashes and paves their way through bushes."

We observe Oxpeckers on the back of the Rhino continuing to graze in front of us. We're told that Rhinos, like Cape Buffalo, are given advance warning of danger by the Oxpeckers' chirring and disturbed movements.

Frightened, Rhinos respond with their own alarm warnings, gasp- puffing. Forewarned, Black Rhino fast trots away from the impending danger with her tail curled over her back and head held high. Adult Rhinos have few successful predators. They fiercely protect their young from hyenas and lions. White Rhino mothers have a close bond, ensuring the safety of their young. When alarmed, White Rhino companions press their hindquarters together and face in different directions. Their defense is accompanied with snarling graduating into a high intensity shriek. Threatened, they raise their heads with cocked ears and eyes glaring at the threat or opponent. They wipe horns angrily on the ground and feint an attack.

Enemies for the Black Rhinos are rare. Lions and packs of wild dogs may foolishly dare to attack a weakened animal or a stray calf. Black Rhinos have been daringly attacked and killed by enraged female elephants without fear. White Rhinos have no predators. Stray calves are easy prey if large predators dare the wrath of an enraged protective Rhino mother. Rhino's worse enemy, man, is one they can't intimidate and defeat.

Patrick says, "Rhinos are capable of successfully defending themselves against predators. All but their worst enemy, man, leave them alone. Man is decimating their population by butchering them for their horns to sell and their heads for trophies. Rhinos, like their mammalian relatives, cannot escape man's lethal snares, traps, and guns. That calf over there will not survive as an orphan. He'll either be food for his predators or die from starvation and dehydration."

We hope that fate will not befall him and wonder whether the lonely calf we're observing has playmates. Patrick reminds us that Black Rhinos are solitary. Sadly, their calves rarely have playmates. Unlike the Black Rhino female, the White Rhino females and young are sociable and associate in groups. Similar to the Black Rhino, White Rhino females are accompanied by their recently born calf and one or more unrelated calves whose maternal ties ended abruptly after the birth of their new sibling. Calf less White Rhino cows associate in pairs and are tolerant of orphans. Juveniles may live with a couple of cows. The juveniles prefer to associate with peers of their sex and age. These stable herds number up to six Rhinos. The mother and calf in front of us have not rejoined their group in her home range. We watch a solitary calf frolic and toss vegetation for amusement. When the calf is ready to return to his mother's group, he'll calf romp with other juveniles and adolescents. Play chases are accompanied with gruff squealing. Calves prance and head toss during their play. Subadults practice horn wrestling preparing for adulthood. The horn wrestling prepares them as adults when they'll meet each other in an intimidation ritual. A pair of males meeting each other crosses their horns. They are testing each other's strength and promptness of the other's reflexes. If they end up fighting, they stop at a certain point without either one being injured.

White Rhino   Photo by Dorothy Van Horn

During our drive back to camp for lunch, James points at a group of White Rhinos of females, calves, and adolescents. Their heads appear to be attached permanently to the ground as they graze hungrily on the short, green grass.

We're told that James found an area near our lodge where the nocturnal Rhino Beetles may be observed. We're instructed to meet after dinner. Since it'll be cold and dark, we'll told to dress warmly and bring flashlights for our night's adventure.

CHAPTER 6

PINCERS - THE RHINOCEROS BEETLE

Orcytes rhinoceros

After dinner, the adventurous and hardier members of our group meet James and Patrick to find another member of the Little Five, the Rhinoceros Beetle. James leads us on a short walk from our dining room to a wooded area near a couple of our lodges. Earlier, he saw beetles scurrying in litter under trees.

Along the way, Patrick tells us that Rhino Beetles are mostly nocturnal; they're most active at night. They like to forage, eat, crawl around, party, and mate during the night. Adult Rhinos dine on sap and rotting food. In spite of their size, they don't eat much.

Photo by Hal Brindley, travel l4 wildlife

During the day they hide under logs or vegetation. They have few predators large enough who want to devour them. We have flashlights because the beetles we are seeking are difficult to find in the dark. Their black, heavy armor camouflage them in the night's darkness. Rhinoceros Beetles are heavy weight relatives of the famous Egyptian scarab beetle. The Rhino Beetle is the largest of all beetles in the world. They're larger and heavier than many birds. The Rhino Beetle measures over two inches in length. In spite of their size, adults do not eat much of the food they feed on – nectar, plant sap and fruit.

Rhino Beetle males are the super heavy weightlifting champs of their insect world. Elephants and ants are reputed to be strong. However, a huge African Elephant can only lift 25% of its own weight onto its back. The elephant is no match for its insect weightlifting rival. A Rhinoceros Beetle can carry 850 times its own weight. That would be comparable to an elephant carrying 850 elephants on his back! Competing with the Rhino Beetle, an average weight and height human with the Beetle's strength would only be able to lift a 65-ton object. If we humans could match the Rhino Beetle's strength, we'd be carrying our cars instead of riding in them. Rhinoceros Beetles are the strongest animals on the planet, proportionally.

Patrick points his flashlight at the shiny black armor of a male Rhinoceros Beetle. He's attempting to escape from us by vigorously digging under heavy litter to burrow underground. We watch him as Patrick informs us about this insect member of the Little Five.

They're called Rhinoceros Beetles because they have horns like Rhinoceros. Unlike the Rhinoceros, where both females and males have horns, only male beetles have long, large horns. Females of the *Orcytes rhinoceros* are less intimidating as they do not have horns like their male counterparts. They are plain and less frequently seen than horned males.

The Rhinoceros Beetle has several other names. He's known as the Hercules Beetle, Elephant Beetle, Unicorn Beetle and Horn Beetle. Since he's the little counterpart of the Big Five's Rhinoceros, we prefer to refer to him as the Rhinoceros Beetle.

Male Rhinoceros Beetles appear fierce but are harmless members of the insect world. Their horns are incapable of biting or stinging humans. One horn project from his head, the other extends forward from the middle of his thorax. Each of his horns is slightly forked at its end. The two horns almost meet each other. By moving his head, a male beetle can manipulate them like pincers. Horns are used in mating battles against other males vying to court females of their choice. They battle each other for dominant supremacy like most of the male animals we've seen.

When threatened, Rhino Beetles escape danger by using their horns to dig and burrow into the underground. Their best protection from predators is their large size combined with being nocturnal. Their fearsome large, shiny black, horned appearance is enhanced by loud hissing squeaks when threatened or disturbed. Their vocalization is an intimidating bluff. Sounds are produced by rubbing their abdomen against the ends of their wing covers. Patrick tells us that he was curious and once examined a squeaking beetle. He inspected it closely and watched the beetle's abdomen moving in sequence with its squeaks.

Patrick segues into the mating behavior of the Rhinoceros Beetle. "Rhino Beetles have distinct sexes, male and female. These beetles reproduce sexually during the rainy season. A female comes of age when she's older than one month when her ovaries are filled with full-sized eggs."

Patrick describes the odd mating ritual of Rhinoceros Beetles. During the mating season, males are very belligerent and aggressive. Interested in attracting a female they battle over a feeding site of litter. By securing a feeding site, the victorious male attracts a female and wins the privilege of mating with her. Clashing males wave their horns up and down, attempting to grab each other. Manipulating their horns like calipers, a wrestler scoops up his opponent's body tossing him away from the treasured feeding site. Like a sumo wrestler, the raging warrior uses his long, well-armed front legs to viciously rake his competitor. The opponents ram each other with their large horns and knock each other tumbling over the litter. Clashing giants accompany their conflict with constant belligerent chirping. Finally, the victorious winner announces his conquest by vigorously chirping. Attracted by his excited chirping, a female approaches her conquered territory. She attracts him with her secretion of pheromones proclaiming her willingness to mate. Her goliath mounts on top of her. If he slips from her smooth back, he clasps her wrapping his legs around her thorax. Their love making may continue for several hours. During their mating, sperm is transferred from the male to the female. After fertilizing her eggs, her mate unceremoniously leaves her to fend on her own. During a warmer and less rainy season, a fertilized female deposit 50 tiny, oval, white eggs under the feeding site's ground.

Photo by Michael Wilcox, unsplash

After laying her eggs, the mother leaves them to develop on their own. Eggs she's laid are not safe. A mite living underground where the eggs are left feeds on them. The mite is about the same size as the Rhino beetle's eggs. Another predator of the beetle's eggs is the maggot of the Midas fly. The maggot digs into the ground and devours the Rhino Beetle's eggs. By devouring eggs of the Rhino Beetle, mites and maggots are controlling the Beetle's population.

After three weeks to a month, the surviving eggs hatch and develop into larvae. The larval stage lasts for many years, about three to five years before they mature. The larvae are curved, whitish and slow moving. They consume a great deal of food from the feeding site of rotting wood and decaying leaves, food their father won for them. Following several long years, the larva goes through three molts before changing into their third stage of development, the pupae stage.

During the third stage of their complete metamorphosis, a full-grown larva forms a cell in the soil. The cell is lined with feces that solidify into a waterproof layer. While in the cell, the larva changes into a pupa. This change does not take as long as the preceding larva's three molts stage. Larva changing to pupa takes up to nine months. This metamorphosis occurs during the winter.

After hatching from a pupa into an adult beetle during the fourth and final stage of their metamorphosis, the adult remains underground until spring. Then an adult beetle digs a way out to the surface. Rhino Beetle's cycle of life continues with them feeding and mating. If the adult is a female, she will find and attract a mate by releasing pheromones. After a successful mating, she lays her eggs beginning another generation of Rhinoceros Beetles. The life span of this species of Rhinoceros Beetle is not certain. The life span varies with the 300 various types of Rhino Beetle species. It may range from weeks to months.

Patrick bleakly states the problems faced by all African animals, including the Rhinoceros Beetle. "Human's greed is impacting the Rhinoceros Beetle and all animals throughout Africa. Continued deforestation, destruction of forests and slash and burning of vegetation will cause the disappearance and extinction of these goliath beetles from planet earth. We won't see Rhinoceros Beetles in their natural habitat as we are tonight. We Africans could, as the Asians do, maintain their existence by keeping them as pets. The Rhinoceros Beetles, not of the *Orcytes rhinoceros* species, are popular pets in Asia. We could, like the Asians, breed our Rhinoceros Beetle for gambling fights. Gamblers bet on male beetles competing over female beetles. The winner is determined when he knocks his opponent off the log where the fight is staged. Maintaining our Rhinoceros Beetles as pets or fighters is a poor option. It's best that animals of all species live, mate, and breed in their natural habitat. A better alternative is to discourage man's destructive impact on Mother Nature.

We need to conscientiously protect all threatened wildlife by conservation of their natural resources. It's not too late to encourage preserving the African wildlife's habitat. We must do so or most, if not all, of them will be further endangered. It's too late for some of our wildlife that once roamed our savannas and woodlands. Unfortunately, they are now extinct."

We're shocked to hear that even an insect may be threatened by mankind. We return thoughtfully to the camp's observation deck for a night cap. In the lounge, we notice a Rhinoceros Beetle flying to a light. Like moths, Rhino Beetles are attracted to lights. We're told that they're able to fly because they have a pair of heavy horny wings. The heavy wings protect delicate membranous wings underneath. Unlike the lighter moth, Rhino Beetles are not good flyers because of their weight.

During our night cap and snacks, Patrick prepares us for our morning game drive. "Tomorrow morning we'll be searching for two of the Big Five. We heard one of them, a lion roaring, during our afternoon drive the first day. The leopard is very elusive. Hopefully, we'll be able to spot him. We also have two remaining members of the Little Five, the Ant Lion and Leopard Tortoise. On our walking safari we saw the openings to tunnels dug by the Ant Lion. Like the Leopard, the Ant Lion is secretive and difficult to find. Maybe we'll be lucky and see all five of the Big and Little animals on your wish list."

CHAPTER 7

SOCIAL - THE LION

Panthera leo

We leave our camp immediately after our early breakfast. Our group is enthusiastically anticipating spotting the largest of the African predators, the majestic Lion. We're assured by Patrick that we'll have a better opportunity of seeing the most sociable of the cats, the Lion, than the elusive, solitary Leopard. Lions are the only wild cats that live socially. We're hoping to see several members of a pride, a family group. We're told that a typical pride consists of a coalition-group of one to six males and four to fifteen females with their young, cubs and juveniles. Remaining in a pride is the basis of their survival and companionship. Lion society is the most cooperative unit of all mammalian species. While in a pride, cubs and youngsters learn rules of interaction and survival tactics from older members. Duties of the pride are strictly divided. Females, the Lionesses hunt. Males remain behind to guard and defend their huge territory and young.

Unlike most animals, there is no pecking order or social hierarchy among Lions. Lions and Lionesses are equal except when they are feeding. Because of their massive power, males are dominant during meals.

Lions rarely stray from their chosen habitat, except during the rainy season when they roam away seeking grass-eating, herbivorous, prey. Our group is fortunate as we're on safari during the dry season. Patrick assures us that we'll find these noble members of the Big Five. However, to be successful, we need to locate their territory.

Lions are most active at sunrise and early evening. Our chances of seeing a Lion pride are enhanced by their sedentary habit of lazing around in the shade or moving sluggishly during the day. We're informed that Lions typically spend twenty to twenty-one hours a day resting. The Lions we are hunting live on the open plains of the savanna on our campsite's reserve.

James holds his hand up signaling Patrick to stop our Land Rover. They both peer at the sandy soil. Patrick and James climb down from our vehicle to inspect the spoor or track of paw prints. They help us down to look at the prints. James and Patrick identify the spoor as that of a male Lion and his consort. Curious, we asked how they could distinguish the differences.

Patrick responds by pointing at two sets of footprints. One set appears to be deeper than the other. We're informed that the deeper set is male. The average weight of a male is 416 pounds. The female's paw print is set lighter. The average weight for a Lioness is 277 pounds. Lions are the largest of Africa's carnivores and are symbols of nobility and courage for the Masai warriors of Kenya.

Photo by Dorothy Van Horn

Returning to our Land Rover, James leans down from his bucket seat pointing at the trail of footprints. Suddenly, he points at a pair of tawny Lions swaggering ahead of us. Ever alert, their massive heads swing side to side. We're told that the male's thick, tawny mane identifies him as a young male. As a male ages, the color of his mane changes from tawny to red brown to black. Only males have shaggy manes increasing his apparent size and giving him an imposing, majestic appearance. His thick mane protects his neck and throat during fights with other males over territory and females. As he ages, like his mane, a male Lion's iris eye-color varies with age from gold to brown.

Photo by Birger Strahl, unsplash

We follow behind the pair. They both have perfectly muscled and proportioned bodies with short coats, a tuft on their tails, and white underparts. Their legs are short with thick, powerful muscles. Due to their immense physical strength, Lions, whether they are hunting alone or as a team, are at the top of the savanna food chain. The lordly Lion has no enemies. Animals are afraid of his prowess. He intimidates those of his species and others with a variety of sounds (roaring, snarling, growling, spitting, and hissing) and formidable facial expressions. When attacked, he paralyzes his assailant by biting into its lower back. He kills his enemy by crushing its skull. Men are the Lions' only enemy. Lion population is decimated by men hunting them for trophies and competing for their source of food, antelopes. Another enemy is Mother Nature during her drastic periods of drought.

We follow the pair until they disappear into the thick brush. Driving on, we hope that James and Patrick will find a pride that we may stop and observe. In the distance we hear a Lion's full-throated, thunderous roar ending with guttural grunts Patrick explains the roaring. "Since it's in the distance, it's difficult to distinguish whether it's the roar of a male or a female. Most likely it's a male defending his territory and pride. Males begin roaring at one year. Females start to roar a couple of months later. If we were closer, we'd be able to hear the difference between a male's roar from that of a female. His is deeper, vibrant, and louder than that of a female. Remember hearing a Lion roar during our first sundowner? We heard them roaring about five to eight miles from us. Evenings, nights, and shortly before dawn are peak times when they are active and roaring at varying decibels and pitches."

Photo by Dorothy Van Horn

James spots a pride and guides Patrick towards a bare, sandy area backed by thorn bushes and umbrella Acacias. Resting under the shade of the bushes are Lions contentedly purring, humming, and grooming each other. "They sound and are behaving like my cat, Pepper," comments a member of our group. We stop near a pride. There are about eleven members in the family group. Patrick points at and identifies each member.

He says, "That one with the thick, black mane is the dominant male. He has a harem of three adult females, two female subadults, two male juveniles, and three cubs. There is no pecking order among those females or between the male and females, except while dining. Members of a family group come and go unpredictably. They may go it alone or in groups that number three to five Lions. A large pride of forty never assembles in one place. When members of a pride meet, they perform a ritual beginning with nose sniffing, followed by rubbing their heads and sides against each other. They drape their erect tail with its tip over the member they're greeting."

Photo by Dorothy Van Horn

We're told that the females in the group in front of us are related. Mothers, daughters, cousins and granddaughters form a pride based on kinship. They're territorial and gregarious. Females are attached to their birthplace and reluctantly leave when it's overcrowded. By departing from their familiar family area, they leave behind crucial knowledge of their hunting grounds. Seeking prey in their new habitat will be difficult until they adapt and learn where to readily find game.

Family members cooperate in raising young and sharing prey. A female not belonging to the pride is ostracized and chased away. The intruder is identified by her lack of self-assurance to meet and greet the members of a group. This signals that she is not a member of their family. As an intruder she's banished.

Patrick tells us that, "The older, dominant male will drive that young juvenile male away when he reaches two or three years old. Unwanted, he'll either roam alone or join a small male coalition. He or his small group will wander until they find a pride of females they can control. If the pride has an aging male, the youngsters will fight, chasing him away or killing him to win his reigning position."

As we're observing the family group, we notice a nervous, hyperactive female frantically rubbing against objects and rolling on the dirt. She approaches the male, seductively purrs and sinuously rubs against him.

Patrick exclaims, "You're in luck! She's advertising that her estrus is beginning. She's in heat and ready to mate. He's in for several fights because she's blatantly advertising her willingness to mate to all males who may be in the vicinity."

"As I mentioned earlier, a victorious male who drives away a reigning male or kills him takes over the loser's pride. The conqueror slaughters all the vanquished ruler's cubs under a year old. Older juveniles may escape but must do so with their mothers or they can't survive without them. By ridding the pride of cubs and juveniles the new monarch ensures that his genes are inherited. When the cubs were alive and healthy, females in the pride were infertile. Upon their young's infanticide, females ovulate, begin their estrus, and copulate with their new consort."

Patrick continues describing mating behavior among Lions. "The male in front of you has the advantage of size and a thick mane. He is obviously strong and fit - no worries for him as he has mating rights, lasting for two to three years. He'll competently keep competitors at a distance. Leo will lose his reign because of age to a younger and stronger male or to a group of four to six males. There is no dominance among this coalition of males. The gang will outnumber and drive him away. They may also slaughter him. Since there are no roaming males nearby, he'll be able to hold his own. Presently he's in his prime, about five years. He's not losing weight and hair from his mane indicating an age of eight years or older. By his tenth year he'll probably be dead.

While that flirtatious female is beginning her estrus, he'll guard her ensuring that he alone will sire their offspring. All the females in this group will be monopolized for reproduction by him. That monopoly of reproduction is observed only in Lions where there is a pronounced sexual dimorphism – distinct difference between their sexes. Leo has an advantage of large size and a protective mane making him so bulky that he has difficulty hunting. His role is to guard the pride's territory and his offspring while females hunt. Their roles change when he's away guarding their territory. While he's away, his females will fiercely and determinedly protect their young by swiftly attacking, chasing, and cuffing the trespasser.

Patrick educates us about reproduction among Lions. "Lionesses begin breeding at four, a year earlier than males. Following puberty, females are sexually receptive any time throughout the year. There is no breeding season. Breeding is year-round and is synchronized (occurring at the same time) within a pride. Females giving birth in synchrony will communally care for and nurse each other's young. Lioness' estrus lasts about four days with a two-to-three-week interval between cycles.

Females live up to eighteen years, two years longer than males. The interval between births is eighteen to twenty-six months. During those months, females with cubs are infertile. By the fifteenth year, breeding stops. The proximity of those two signify their readiness to mate. We watch the Lioness as her adoring suitor pursues her so closely that he trips on her feet. Patrick says his antics are characteristic of Lion courtship. She rebuffs his advances by snarling and slapping at him. He grimaces when he sniffs her rear attempting to check the state of her estrus. She slowly and reluctantly yields to his amorous attention. No longer coy, she displays her interest and willingness by taking over the initiative. She crouches and presents her rear into his face. Leo mounts her beginning what Patrick refers to as a "sexual marathon."

Patrick describes their mating. "They'll copulate for twenty-one seconds. Like all Lions, those two will mate often at fifteen-minute intervals up to three hundred times. A male Lion has more stamina than other mammals except for Leopards. A dedicated researcher recorded a Lion copulating 157 times during fifty-five hours with two females. While serving the two different females, the Lion's inexhaustible efforts increased to three and a half times per hour."

Photo by David Clode unsplash

Patrick continues, "There is a biological reason for their frequent copulation. Frequency is important as it stimulates ovulation. Scientists discovered that estrus cycles occur for months without ovulation. That explains why only one mating cycle in five results in offspring. Once ovulation occurs, the chances for fertility are very high: 95%. Throughout their sexual encounter, a female is in intense pain caused by the barbs on his penis. Throughout their copulation, she grimaces and continues an ominous rumbling moan from pain and aversion to being uncomfortably straddled. You've heard house-cat males yowling during their mating.

Similarly, a male Lion meows sounding like he's in distress. That meowing crescendos into loud, harsh yowls when he reaches climax; followed by his quick and light biting off the nape of her neck. Immediately after, he moans and hastily jumps away, avoiding her nastily attacking him. While he's attempting to escape, she twists her head with an explosive snarl and attempts to cuff his head. Once he's safely off her, she purrs contentedly and lazily rolls onto her back. Her initial angry unwillingness has turned to sexual pleasure. Wanting another marathon, she follows the retreating, tired Leo. She demonstrates her willingness to mate again by seductively purring and slinking around him. Frustrated, she shakes and slaps her slumbering fatigued Romeo. When he's finally aroused, their mating will continue until he tires of her and searches for another female beginning her estrus. If there is more than one male in a pride, Leo willingly leaves her to enjoy the pleasures of his energetic friend."

Photo by Tom Podmore, unsplash

We're instructed to look at the male's wide flat nose, brow, and cheeks. Patrick explains what we see, "Those deep scratches that you see on Leo are from the claws of his numerous amorous matings. He didn't duck in time!"

"Unlike Elephants' long pregnancies, the gestation period of Lions is a brief 110 days," Patrick remarks. "For every cub that lives until he is a year old, Lions copulate about 3,000 times. A pregnant Lioness leaves her pride to give birth in solitude. She returns to her pride when the cubs are six weeks old. At birth a cub weighs 2 to 4.5 pounds, about 1% of an adult's weight. An average litter is two to three tawny, wooly, grayish spotted cubs. There have been litters up to six cubs. Survival rate decreases with an increase in multiple cubs. A mother has only four teats to nurse her young."

Regarding the young, "Like kittens, the newborn is totally helpless. They are blind until their eyes open at three to eleven days. They are deaf and barely able to crawl. They remain in their den until they are mobile. If disturbed, the cubs are carried one at a time by the head, nape, or back skin to another hiding place. When they stray and meow loudly, their mother retrieves and comforts them with vigorous licks. Cubs will begin walking at ten to fifteen days and running at one month. Older cubs are warned to take cover by their mother's hissing and slapping them alerting and teaching the youngsters which animals are to be feared."

I notice patches of black on the meowing cubs. "What are those black spots on their ears and tail?" I inquire.

Patrick replies, "All Lions of all ages have "follow me" black markings on the tip of their ears and tail. After seven weeks of solitude, returning to her pride, cubs follow their mother's and each other's marking. They'll be cared for, nursed, and protected by the pride's females. Fathers have no role in caring for their young. Occasionally fathers allow them to play on or near them. When impatient fathers have enough of their cubs' antics, they'll be snarled at and cuffed away."

Continuing his dialogue, Patrick says, "By seven weeks, cubs can keep up with their family. Remember my mentioning synchronization among the females? Cubs' chances for survival improve when the births of females in the pride occur within the same time. Females suckle one another's young communally. Cubs' rate of survival also increases when there are no older cubs for them to compete with for the milk of nursing females. Newborns suckle from one to ten minutes on the females' four teats. At the age of four months, they suckle about fifteen minutes per day. Although they are weaned about seven to ten months, they remain dependent on their mother and her relatives until they are sixteen months old. They are unable to hunt and fend for themselves before then."

Patrick imparts interesting information regarding parental care. Mothers hide their young cubs and leave them for twenty-four hours to socialize and consort with their pride's females. There are no cub sitters for the little ones. Frightened and alarmed cubs straying from their protective shelter scamper back where they won't be detected. Stray and lost cubs are easy prey for hungry hyenas, cheetahs, and rampaging male Lions from a different pride.

Patrick relates a study by George Schaller. "During Schaller's observations, a mother Lion left her three small cubs under a fallen tree. Two Lions from another pride killed the cubs while she was away. One of her cubs was partially devoured by one of the males. A second male carried another cub away, dangling it not as a cub but as if it were captured food. He licked the dead cub, played with it, and nestled it between his paws. Schaller recorded that he continued his ritual for ten hours and refrained from eating the succumbed cub. The returning mother discovered her third cub lying dead. She licked it, sat down, and ate it. All that was left of her cannibalism were her cub's head and front paws. Who knows what she was feeling, if anything? Possibly she felt closer to her dead offspring when she recycled him into her body. Maybe she was imparting her love for it by devouring it, forever keeping him, or she may have been practicing a funeral rite. It's unfortunate that we humans can't access the minds of animals to better understand them."

Continuing his dialogue, Patrick says, "Obviously, Lionesses are not doting mothers. They don't slow their pace for offspring more than five to seven months old. Nor do they slow down to protect a weak and/or injured cub. Often, a single cub is abandoned and dies from not being able to care for himself. Rather than spending her energy inefficiently raising one cub, that Lioness will use her energy more efficiently by breeding and raising another litter. Whenever food for the Lioness is scarce, cubs are abandoned and left to starve to death. Only when the young are capable of hunting and killing for themselves will the risk of starvation recede. Although it appears that Lioness is a cruel mother, she is stacking the deck for survival of only fit cubs. One of her most important roles as a mother is to protect her young litter. When a pride is taken over by a conquering male, a female will ferociously defend her young from being killed by the invader who's attempting to sire only his generation of genes. A Lioness will protectively rescue and defend her helpless young from ravaging packs of hyenas."

"Regarding the females before you," Patrick expounds, "they'll remain in their family group until they die. Female lifespan may be up to sixteen years of age. If the pride grows too large, some Lionesses may be shunned and chased away or leave on their own and become nomads. Dominant males expel young males of about two to three years old. Homeless males wander widely and have no territory. At five to six years of age, male nomads have grown bulky and developed full, bushy manes. Prime males form an alliance of two to five which often includes brothers or half-brothers. They gang together in driving dominant, established males from their territory. The gang takes over the loser's harem. As I mentioned earlier, all cubs in the pride are slaughtered getting rid of their father's genes and making way for the inheritance of conquerors' gene. Established resident males warn invading males away by vigilantly patrolling, guarding, and scent marking their territory."

"Scent marking is a means of identifying each other. Cubs and older Lions communicate by scent marking and smell. Male Lions are the most active markers; females do so occasionally by squirting urine against vertical objects. Like our male pet dogs, urine spraying is primarily a male Lion's thing. Lions mark their paths by raising their tails and spraying urine that is a mixture of secretion from two anal glands. Other Lions walking in the area sniff marked objects with closed eyes. You've seen dogs rubbing their backs on grass and sniffing marked bushes. Similarly, Leo checks markings by rubbing his face and mane against a sprayed small tree or bush and sniffing. Lions communicate like our domestic dogs; they sniff each other when meeting. Like bloodhounds, another Lion's path is sniffed. Sniffing enables their tracking and finding or avoiding each other.

Scent identifies the Lion leaving his mark and communicates when he passed by. Their markings proclaim ownership of their territory, killed prey, and estrus female. They pay close attention to one another's unique scent, identifying the odor as either a friend or foe."

Patrick adds that there are other means of communication among Lions enabling them to identify family from enemy. Both sexes perform a scuff marking ceremony beginning when they are two years old. They rhythmically tread and forward kick their back feet with claws extended raking the ground two to thirty times. Scuffing and scratching of trees and the ground is like domestic cats scratching our sofas and carpets. Pet cats don't pee and mix their urine with scuff marks like wild cats.

Patrick segues into discussing Lions' stalking and killing for survival. At two and a half months, cubs watch the movement of prey. Prior to having another litter, mothers train their young to fend for themselves. While they are very young, she brings them dead prey. Then the dead are followed by live ones. Frightened at first by the live animal, they soon are attracted and stimulated by its attempts to escape. The cubs' hunting instinct kicks in by running after their victim. Young become independent after hours of practicing and learning to perfect the fatal neck bite. Like all young, they learn from mimicking the adults. While playing they copy their adults' movements of stalking, ambushing, grappling, and strangling to kill prey. Females, the pride's huntress, continue developing their skills by never losing their playfulness. Adult Lions are often frustrated by rambunctious, unschooled cubs while stealthily stalking game. Cubs as old as seven months ruin their elders hunting by thoughtlessly running ahead, meowing, and alerting their prey to danger.

During dry season, Lions' tawny coats are camouflaged by tall golden grass. They're easily spotted upon leaving their cover for the wide-open spaces inhabited by prey. Consequently, Lions choose to hunt at night, dawn, or twilight when they're not readily seen.

Carnivores are opportunists. Lions steal about 12% of their prey from other carnivores who themselves kill only 13% of their own game. Lions prefer hunting less challenging game: the young or old and sick or wounded rather than full grown healthy animals. Their diet is mainly hoofed mammals, Gazelle, Antelope, Giraffe, Wildebeest, Zebra, and young and crippled Elephants and Rhinoceros. Opportunists, Lions prefer scavenging a meal rather than hunting for one. They're chased away from feeding by large packs of ravenous hyenas. During drought when their game is scarce, Lions scavenge on dead animals. They search for rats, fruit, and ostrich eggs. Although they may subsist on this diet until the rainy season, cubs, the old and infirm will die from inability to find food and lack of water. They are recycled by vultures and hyenas.

Photo by Leon Pauleikhoff, unsplash

Some game easily defends themselves with hooves and horns causing serious damage to attacking Lionesses. Larger animals, such as Cape Buffalo, protect themselves by charging after their attackers. Because zebras and wildebeest are bulky compared to the size of Lions, these challenging meals on hooves must be hunted by a large, stealthy, cooperative group. A solitary huntress usually fails and may be seriously injured. When hunting in pairs or solo, one in four hunts is successful. Groups of Lions bag their favorite food, Wildebeests, twice their own weight. Lionesses hunting together aptly kill 80% to 90% of their large prey. Cooperative hunting compensates for the feline's lack of speed (35 miles per hour) compared with the speedier (55 miles per hour) of Gazelles and Zebras. Males participate minimally in the kill but dominant the spoils. When they do hunt, Male Lions are reputed to overcome large prey such as a bull giraffe weighing 2,205 pounds.

Alerted by another ranger radioing Patrick about a kill, we drive rapidly to the area. Our excited group, including myself, has never viewed a kill. We arrive at an awesome scene of a group of Lionesses stealthily stalking a huge Hartebeest (Antelope.) Through our binoculars we watch them creep silently, without detection within sixty to one hundred feet of their quarry. One of the Lionesses dashes out during the last few miles using their weight and power to move swiftly at her top speed. Her sprinting covers the short distance between her and the prey. She catches up to it. Meanwhile, without any signals, her companions circle their victim. One group charges and chases the herd off in the direction of a trap where others are hiding. Another Lioness bounds and leaps obliquely at an angle towards the Hartebeest's rear. Immediately her companions surround their struggling prey. One throws a paw over the beast's shoulder and grips it vise-like in her jaws while another dangles fiercely onto its rump. Cooperatively they use their full weight and strength to yank their quarry down backwards and sideways onto the ground. Another Lioness pounces and lunges onto the fallen animal's exposed throat. She firmly holds onto his throat choking him for thirteen minutes while he struggles to breath. Her companions continue to hang onto him. He finally dies from strangulation. Captivated by the spectacular scenario many of us forget to record an unforgettable photo op.

Patrick comments that if the prey were smaller such as a Wart Hog, one Lioness could efficiently bring him down by slapping his haunch, tripping or clutching him with both of her paws. Then she'd drag it down and quickly slaughter him with a bite to his neck or throat.

Hartebeest   Photo by Chris Stenger, unsplash

We're fascinated by the Lionesses' scrambling, feeding frenzy. Socially they share their kill with the old and crippled members of their pride. Hectic scrambling and competition is characteristic of a Lion society lacking an accepted rank hierarchy. We grumble angrily when their pride's bulky male flaunts his dominance during meals by shouldering and usurping females away from the carcass. He prefers to eat their kill 75% of the time rather than hunting on his own. He's reminiscent of human societies where males feed prior to wives who prepared their meals. The Lion growls, snarls and slaps Lionesses away from the game they stalked, hunted and successfully killed. Suddenly he yanks and tears a hind leg from the carcass and disappears with it into a nearby bush.

Lionesses leave while he's feeding voraciously. They return with hungry cubs. At first the cubs are intimidated and driven away by other Lionesses' harsh snarls and gorging growls typically heard during a feeding orgy. Determined to appease their rumbling stomachs, the cubs timidly return to and grab bites from the Hartebeest. When game is scarce during drought due to global climate changes, cubs are the first to suffer and starve. Mothers will not share their food until they have eaten their fill of eleven to fifteen pounds of meat. Often there is nothing left for the hungry youngsters. We're told that if there is anything left over, Lions will stay and guard their meal from other scavengers, vultures and hyenas. Large packs of hyenas with snapping powerful jaws, intimidate, and drive away Lionesses and cubs. If their consort is present, he'll explosively roar, drawing air deep into his chest, forcing and compressing air into his abdomen, and then out through his vocal cords. His four bellows are followed by a number of grumbling grunts. He leaps towards the hyenas and victoriously chases them away from scavenging his family's dinner.

The engorged cats roll over and rest under the shade of an Acacia tree. Patrick observes their full bellies saying that those felines ate their fill, fourteen pounds of meat. With full bellies they won't hunt for another week. The cats are busily grooming sticky blood off companion's facial hair and whiskers. Patrick explains that they are licking each other scrapping with tongues covered with horned papilla (pimple-like projection.) They sound like house cats purring contently, however Lionesses' purrs are louder and not as frequent. And like domestic cats, Lions rub their cheeks and bodies affectionately together. Mothers and their young are in constant close bodily contact. Several of the cubs and a few adults are playing and romping. We're fortunate to observe these social activities that are more noticeable during evenings and sunrise when these majestic animals are sleeping, hunting, or eating.

It's time for our own feeding frenzy. We return to camp for lunch. Shortly after, we'll meet Patrick on the observation deck. There we'll learn about Leo's tiny counterpart, the solitary Ant Lion.

CHAPTER 8

SOLITARY - THE ANT LION

Myrmeleontidae

We gather on the observation deck overlooking the camp's waterhole. While we wait for the group to convene, we observe two baby elephants playing and rolling in the water. Adults are sucking water with their trunks and depositing it into open mouths. A Lioness and her thirsty cubs are lapping water like our domestic cats. Their tongues aren't as efficient, so they're spending long minutes quenching their thirst. After lapping his fill of water, we watch a well-fed Leo fall asleep near the water's edge.

Photo by Jeremy Pagden unsplash

The Ant Lion is a member of the Little Five. We've seen two of the five, the Red-Bill Buffalo Weaver and the Rhino Beetle. During our walking safari, Patrick identified hollows in the sand. They were craters of Ant Lions' pits. Their occupants' bristly jaws were poking out from their hideaways. Maybe we'll see the rest of this Little Five's body before our safari ends.

www.shutterstock.com · 567394741

Photo by shutterstock

Patrick begins his lecture about Ant Lions, the Big Five Lion's tiny, solitary counterpart.

"Ant Lions are insects classified as *Myrmeleontidae*, the largest group of the 'Lacewing' family. Ant Lions are misidentified by many as Dragonflies. *Myrmeleontidae* is from the Greek "myrmex" meaning Ant and "leo" meaning Lion. *Myrmeleontidae* is the largest genus of Ant Lions with 158 described species. They belong to the most primitive order, Neuroptera or net wings, of insects with complete metamorphosis (a striking transformation.) The Ant Lion is an insect larva resembling a beetle. Not to confuse you, I'll henceforth refer to the larval stage as Ant Lion or Ant Lion Larva and the adult as an Ant Lion Adult during our discussion."

Patrick continues describing the tiny creature. "The Ant Lion is predacious. It is a mottled gray. She is a grotesque, ferocious looking, wingless insect. Her robust body bears three pairs of short walking legs. Perched on her soft, bristly, rotund body is a slender neck topped with a small head weighed down by a pair of enormous sickle-like, spiny jaws, mandibles. She's sometimes called Sand Dragon. In South Africa, we refer to them as 'Shuntie' and 'Joerie' (pronounced 'Yoory'.) In the United States, you know her best by her familiar nickname, 'Doodlebug.' She earned that moniker by the patterns she designs while searching for an ideal location to dig a tunnel. While meandering, she leaves an odd winding spiraling trail in the sand. Her doodling resembles that of a preoccupied person such as your doodling during a phone conversation."

We gather around a terrarium containing dry, loose sand. During our walking safari, we weren't aware that James had surreptitiously collected several Ant Lions. Patrick removes an Ant Lion from a container. While placing her on the sand, he says:

"James had no problem catching these Ant Lion larvae. They are easy to catch and maintain in captivity. In spite of their fearsome appearance, they are not a serious threat to humans. Ant Lion larvae are too small (half an inch long - about the length of your fingernail) to bite your fingers. Since you're larger than their favorite prey, Ants, you have no fear of being dragged into their sandy trap. She's more in danger of losing her trap when you unknowingly walk onto it. Did you notice what happened when I picked her up and placed her in the terrarium? Once on the sandy soil, since I disturbed her, she covered herself with a layer of sand and is remaining motionless hoping that she'll be overlooked. Ant Lions are great pets and relatively easy to care for as long as they are kept in a container of soft, dry sand with an ample food supply of small, crawling insects."

We chuckle as our Ant Lion doodles and scribbles while meandering on the terrarium's soft sand. She continues searching until she finds the right place to dig. She marks the chosen site by grooving a circle in the sand. Crawling backwards in circles, her head digs a conical pit in the sand. Simultaneously her large jaws toss grains of sand away from her excavation. Each time she moves round and round, her trap gradually grows deeper and deeper. The result of her tedious efforts is a crater of two inches deep and three inches wide at its edge. The crater's walls are very steep. She designs the crater of her pit with a sloping funnel. Patrick explains that the slope is crucial. It's fashioned at a critical angle of repose (the steepest angle the sand can maintain where the slightest disturbance will cause it to collapse.) The angle is such that the sides will readily give way under her unsuspecting prey's feet preventing it from escaping.

We comment that the pit looks like a crater or top of an ice cream cone. We observe the Ant Lion as she tunnels into her excavation.

Patrick informs us that she's concealing herself. "She's waiting quietly there with her body off to one side. The steep wall conceals her."

We notice only her sickle like jaws protruding from the sand. The jaws are wide open and ready for an unsuspecting prey.

"Watch what happens next," instructs Patrick. He picks up another container and pours a couple of ants from a vial into the terrarium.

We watch the ants scramble looking for shelter. One of the ants is curious. It looks down into the bottom of the pit. It continues staring seemingly mesmerized by the pit's conical shape. We wonder whether it's fascinated by the shape or possibility of food at the pit's bottom. After a few minutes of indecision, to satisfy his curiosity, he proceeds to cautiously test the smooth and steep banks with his forelegs. As soon as he steps over the pit's edge, the treacherous sand gives way. The startled ant struggles to regain his foothold, stumbling, and dislodging more sand. Slipping and sliding, he falls into the waiting, hungry jaws of the Ant Lion. Curiosity killed the ant. The Ant Lion's industry and ingenuity is rewarded.

The other ant is not as deadly curious as his unfortunate companion. He is wandering perilously on a side of the pit where he decides he's unsafe and in danger. We watch as he slips and slides trying to leave the sandy side of the trap for safer ground. He turns around and attempts to climb up away from the precipitous side. His efforts unsettle the sand causing it to immediately roll down the pit's side. The falling sand immediately alerts the Ant Lion. She quickly hurls showers of sand upwards causing the startled ant to fall downwards. The Ant Lion seizes her fallen prey with her formidable jaws.

Patrick comments. "There is no escape for her trapped victim. The projections on the side of her jaws are hollow. They're like hypodermic needles. She sucks away the juices of her prey while she's holding it. Those ants were an easy meal for her. Observe what happens when I place this large Dung Beetle near the pit's side."

The Dung Beetle loses his foothold on the slippery sand and falls onto the pit's bottom. He is more of a challenge for the ravenous Ant Lion. Moving desperately to escape and survive, the Dung Beetle struggles away from his predator. He cleverly piles grains of sand into a mound that will allow him to climb out of the pit. Trying to escape from his predator's vicious jaws, he frantically scrambles towards the pit's top. His valiant efforts fail as the smaller Ant Lion triumphantly captures him.

Patrick explains the small larva's actions. "Her entire body is covered in stiff bristles that anchor her in the sand while he's attempting to escape. Those bristles are forward pointing providing additional leverage to firmly anchor her against his vigorous struggles. The doomed victim is pulled down beneath the sand as massive jaws clamp over him. Her mandibles are piercing and sucking her prey. After she seizes the Beetle, she paralyzes it with poison injected during her first bite. Following the toxin are digestive enzymes that breakdown the internal tissues of the Dung Beetle's cumbersome body. The injected enzymes liquefy his body. All that is left from her feast is his exoskeleton. Watch her tidy her home. The gorged Ant Lion sweeps her abode clean by unceremoniously tossing her victim's remains out of her pit. We watch as she clears away the mound the beetle built and repairs her trap for another unsuspecting victim."

Patrick compares the Ant Lion with another Little Five. "Unlike Red-Billed Buffalo Weavers, Ant Lions are excellent housekeepers. If small objects like pebbles or bits of leaves fall into her abode, she'll tidy her home by flicking them out like that Beetle's remains. Also, unlike the Red-Billed Weavers, The Ant Lion is an ingenious architect and a precision builder. She designs her trap to efficiently capture her prey and prevent its probability of escaping. She shapes the diameter of her pit to ascertain the probability of capturing prey. Further, she augments the trap with a steep slope and great depth increasing the probability of trapping her victim. Ant Lions are masters of survival under the worse conditions. If their traps of sand are destroyed by wind, rain, animals, or vehicles, they calmly rebuild and patiently wait for their next meal. Entomologists (scientists who study insects) maintain that the Ant Lions survival throughout enumerable centuries is due to their ingenuity and perseverance."

"Ant Lions are one of the most fascinating and cleverest of insect predators. They're beneficial to humans because of their diet." Patrick adds. "The Larva gets rid of common pests. They are famous for feeding on and helping to remove pesky Ants, including dreaded, imported Fire Ants. As the Larvae increase in size, they're capable of capturing and slaying a variety of other insects that are foolish to enter their traps. Besides beetles, they devour crickets and small spiders. Ant Lions are unusual insects. They lack an anus. Wastes are stored in their larval bodies. They immediately dispose their wastes when they emerge from their pupae as adults.

shutterstock.com · 1756841282

Ant Lion Larva   Photo by shutterstock

Continuing his lecture, Patrick states that Ant Lions live a solitary existence. As larva they do not and cannot mate until they undergo complete metamorphosis (transformation) from larvae to pupae and then to adulthood. The larva in front of us will grow as she continues to suck and feed on her prey's fluid through those hollow projections in her jaws. Depending on her food supply, she may spend two years remaining in her trap and hunting as a larva. When she's increased her size and changes into a pupa, she'll spin a circular cocoon of mucus and sand around her body. The cocoon is spun several inches below the sand. Upon completion of her cocoon, she'll transform into a pupa. As a pupa, she'll remain in her cocoon for a month until she metamorphosizes into a sexually mature insect. As an adult she pushes her way through the wall of her sand cocoon and pulls herself up towards its surface. Her pupal case and skin are left behind as she makes her way out of the pit. After twenty minutes, the beautiful Ant Lion's net-wings are fully open. As an adult, an Ant Lion is larger than her larval stage. Her adult exoskeleton is extremely thin, and flimsy compared to her bulkiness as a larva.

She has two pair of long, narrow, multi-veined wings and a long, slender abdomen on her frail adult body. Her wingspan is 6.3 inches. Ant Lion wings are spotted or blotched with black or brown. Ant Lion adults resemble Dragonflies but belong to a different class of winged insects. Both have similar predatory, well-developed jaws. However, unlike their distant relative, Ant Lion adults have prominent clubbed antennae. The antennae are as long as the head and thorax combined. Dragonflies are strong flyers; in contrast, Ant Lions are extremely feeble fliers. Dragonflies are diurnal (day) and Ant Lions are nocturnal, further distinguishing the two.

Patrick reminds us, "When our Ant Lion completes her metamorphosis, she'll deposit the waste she stored during her larval stage. As soon as she's capable, she'll flutter away in search of a mate. Since she's nocturnal, it's not easy to find one in the pitch dark. Adults are attracted to lights increasing her chances of meeting a mate on a lighted sign, streetlight, or lit window screen. Look for them tonight when you return to your lodge. They may be flying around your porch light. If one happens to land on you, don't panic. They're completely harmless. Maybe you'll be fortunate to see a pair mating."

Patrick describes the adults' mating behavior. "The two are like acrobats. Hanging and clinging to a twig, a female attracts a male by exuding her sex pheromone (chemical.) Her mate attaches his tail to hers. He hangs below her suspended only by his genital apparatus. Their copulation lasts for two hours. When they separate, she'll tidy up by feeding on sperms that missed her genital opening. Once again, the life cycle of Ant Lions begins with her egg laying or 'oviposition.' When she finds a suitable place in warm sand, she'll repeatedly tap its surface with the tip of her abdomen. After fashioning a tiny opening among the grains of sand, she then inserts her abdomen into it and lays an egg. She'll repeat this procedure several times in the same sandy area. She'll lay about twenty eggs in each of her twenty depositories. During each oviposition, she raises her wings and fans them rapidly with short wing strokes. Completely her egg laying, she'll return to another twig and will mate again. Adult Ant Lions life span may be more than forty-five days. The laying female must be cautious. If she is near her larval offspring's pits, they'll capture and devour her shortening her life to twenty-five days or less."

Listening to Patrick and watching his fascinating Ant Lion demonstration in the sand terrarium, we agreed that this solitary member of the Little Five is a survivor. Although its longevity is brief, this tiny creature lives a full and fulfilling life.

We'll reconvene for our game drive late this afternoon. Patrick informs us that we'll have a better opportunity to see the last member of the Big Five, the carnivorous Leopard, at dusk. Maybe we'll be lucky to find the Leopard's little counterpart, the herbivorous Leopard Tortoise. If not, we'll have to locate both animals during our last game drive tomorrow morning.

CHAPTER 9

CARNIVOROUS - THE LEOPARD

Panthera pardus

We are on a quest for a stealthy, secretive, and powerful feline, a Leopard. As Patrick drives our Land Rover past dense tall grass and bushes, we sweep our binoculars over the largest of Africa's spotted cats' favorite hideouts. We're searching for the carnivorous Leopard, the Prince of Stealth, at one of his most active periods, dusk. Patrick comments that our chances of finding him are good. We pass trees where we hope to see a Leopard draped over a branch. He's the last member on our list of Big Five; we've seen all five except this solitary creature.

Photo by Irene Shibata

While looking for the elusive, wandering Leopard, we are informed that he is Africa's largest spotted cat. Resting during the day, in dense undergrowth or tree branches, this graceful and powerful beast begins his activity at dusk and is most active at night and a couple hours after dawn. His prominent, sensitive whiskers identify him as an animal that hunts at night. He marks his territory with a scent exuded from his facial glands. Other big cats: Lion, Tiger, Jaguar, and Snow Leopard are his relatives of the genus, *Panthera*.

Patrick instructs us to look for his coat with characteristic spots of bold, dark rosettes (rose-shaped) against a lighter base. "His mottled coat," Patrick says, "provides superb camouflage while he rests during the day and hunts in the night's dim light. Unfortunately, that beautiful coat is the reason he is illegally poached. Throughout the decades, his soft dense, gorgeous fur has been used for ceremonial robes and coats. Man is his primary enemy. His claws, tails, and whiskers are popular fetishes sold for their magical powers by witchdoctors."

Suddenly, James holds his hand up for us to be quiet. Patrick turns off the Rover's engine. We all strain to hear what our tracker's keen ears hear.

I detect an interval of hoarse, rasping coughing. I whisper a question, "Patrick is someone sawing wood in those tall bushes protected by a rocky outcrop at the base of those sausage trees?"

Patrick replies, "Those sounds are what alerted James. That's a Leopard advertising his presence. Let's drive closer to those bushes to search for him or her."

James is seated on his perch over the Rover's right front bumper. He's sweeping the bushes and trees with a floodlight. The light will spot the Leopard's long, low-slung 77-143 pound, 24-28-inch-high body with short muscular limbs. If we find a female, Patrick tells us that she's lighter, 62-128 pounds and a few inches shorter, 23-26 inches.

We see two spots of yellow light from a thick bush in front of us. Patrick exclaims, "We're fortunate those spotted lights are from a Leopard's eyes. Most of my guests are disappointed as this shy, elusive animal is difficult to find. Most of our camp's visitors see the Elephant, Cape Buffalo, Rhino, and Lion but not the fifth member of the Big Five, the Leopard. By James' spotlight stimulating a reflection from that Leopard's eyes, we should be able to find him."

A member of my group inquires, "What's he doing?"

Patrick said, "We've disturbed his attempts to feed. He's dragging that Impala up into that sausage tree's branches to protect his kill. The canopy of Leopards' favorite tree provides perfect concealment. Reclining on the branches of sausage trees, Leopards have a perfect ambush. From their perch, clever Leopards pounce on unsuspecting prey grazing below them. These large spotted cats spend two thirds of their lives slumbering sprawled in thick undergrowth or on tree branches shading them from the sun."

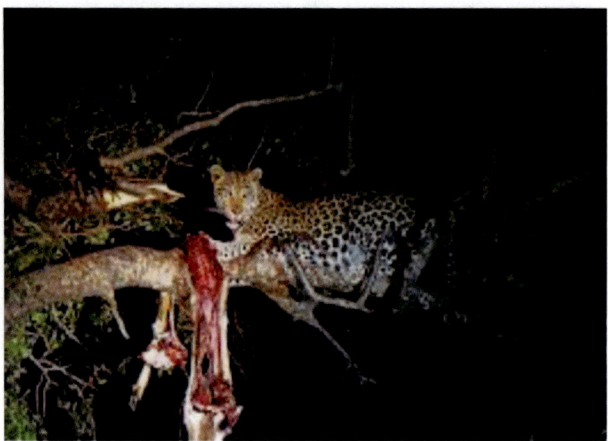

Photo by Joe McDaniel unsplash

Wow! I exclaim, "what are those eerie looking yellow lights coming from his eyes?" I've seen red eye spots from camera flashes, but never yellow spots. Those glowing eyes remind me of vampire movies!"

Patrick answers, "Have you ever flashed a light at your dog's or cat's eyes or seen photographs of them taken with a flash? You may have noticed their eyes as bright yellow spots. All animals, except humans, have a reflective membrane, Tapetum lucidum, lining the back of their eyes. Nocturnal animals have this reflective membrane. It acts like a mirror and reflects light back through their retina. Tapetum lucidum gives the retina two chances to catch light, going in and out of their eyes, enabling animals to see clearer in dark areas. Bright light is not necessary for them to see. Tapetum increases the likelihood of dim light stimulating the rods and cones in animals' eyes. Animals have more rods for night vision and cones for color and day vision than we do. We eat carrots to improve our poor night vision. Leopards are carnivorous and don't eat carrots. Their eyesight is outstanding and excels ours. Their night vision is awesome. It's six times better than ours. Outstanding night vision enables predators to see their prey and prey to see predators. As you know, the Leopard is a carnivorous predator. Watch his eyes when James flashes the light at his eyes. Notice the light's reflection is coming from his eyes that are close together. Due to the set closeness of their eyes, all predators have a direct line of sight to their prey. Later, we'll look for a herd of Impalas and flash our light at them. All prey, like the Impala he killed lying under him, have eyes that are wide apart for excellent all-around vision. The set of their eyes enable them to see their surroundings and bolt from approaching enemies.

Photo by Jane Stroebel, unsplash

As we drive and stop near the reclining Leopard, Patrick radios other rangers informing them of our Leopard sighting. No more than three Land Rovers may be near any sighting. We are close enough to hear the rasping of this timid, skittish cat's tongue as he grooms himself. Not wanting to disturb and scare him away, we quietly watch him. Besides excellent eyesight, Leopard's possess keen hearing. He may have heard us. He suddenly leaves his haven, dragging the bulky Impala with him towards the trees.

We're all startled and delighted to see two cubs climbing out of their hideaway in the rocky outcrop. They scramble and follow the adult Leopard's follow me sign, a white tipped tail. Our Leopard is not a male! We've found a female with two cubs! We watch the trio climb the tree. The Leopardess drags her kill upwards and drapes it on a high branch. The power of her claws, leg and neck muscles are awesome. Panting from her exertion, she sprawls, resting on the broad branch. After a brief rest period, she begins feeding by tearing tufts from the Impala's fur. Once a patch of flesh is exposed, she begins feeding on her precarious perch. We watch her bite into the Impala's flesh with her powerful, muscular jaws. She tears and stabs into its meat with long, pointed, vicious canines. What she doesn't devour is saved for a later meal.

Patrick comments that her cubs are about six months old. They are also tearing at the Impala's exposed flesh. He explains the reason for the Leopardess' awkward feeding position.

"Leopards are powerful and extremely strong animals. They are outstanding hunters. Their spotted coats enable them to blend into bush, dappled shade, and under trees. Their excellent camouflage enables them to mysteriously and uncannily disappear while in full view. That's why they are difficult to find. That sausage tree is her vantage point. She has a 360-degree view of her surroundings. It's a resting and feeding place for her. She's dragged that Impala up into those high branches to protect it from scavenging packs of Hyenas, Wild Dogs, and Lions."

"The thrill of watching Leopards hunt never wanes for me. It's exciting and invigorating. Like our domestic cats stalking mice, Leopards are capable of quietly and patiently stalking prey. They attempt to get within five yards of a victim before pouncing and taking their meal by complete surprise. A stalking Leopard springs at and pounces on her quarry from a maximum distance of twenty yards. Desperate for food, she'll sprint and try to go beyond her maximum and go fifty yards. If she misses, even though she's capable of speeding up to thirty-seven miles per hour, she'll quit her chase. Lions rush their prey, Leopards pounce on theirs. Although her major prey is small and medium sized antelope, like that 150-pound Impala she recently killed, she is tremendously strong and can handle their size. She can successfully annihilate an animal twice her size. I've seen Leopards pull down and stranglehold a three-hundred-pound adult Kudu and Wildebeest and drag her kill to the safety of trees. Other preys are Bush Pigs, Wart Hogs, and Jackals. Baboons are Leopards favorite food. However, they run into serious trouble if they foolishly and openly attack a member of a protective Baboon troop. Domestic dogs are also at the top of the spotted felines' meat market list. A silent, bold, crafty Leopard easily abducts sleeping dogs from their owner's doorsteps. When food is scarce due to drought, man's slash and burn tactics, and global climate change, Leopards will hunt unusual fare: snakes, porcupines, fish, domestic stock, guinea fowl, rats, and mice. Hungry Leopards will scavenge on dead animals when their favorite food is not available."

Kudu   Photo by Jamie Muller, unsplash

"Those cubs you see clinging to the tree's branch are about six months or older. They've been weaned and learned to enjoy the meat from their mother's kill. When they are old enough to fend for themselves, she'll send them away. By doing so, she'll go into estrus and be ready to mate again."

We listen to Patrick's explanation of Leopards mating that is very similar to that of Lions and most felines. Unlike social Lions, Leopards are antisocial. They prefer ranging on their own. Males' home ranges may overlap with territories of females, but they carefully avoid each other. The only exception is when a solitary male's mating instinct overcomes his antisocial behavior. He'll search for a female beginning her estrus. They'll consort with each other, mating and hunting together for a week. When mating ceases, each Leopard returns once again to their solitary life.

Reaching maturity at two years of age, Leopards begin mating. Like Lions, there is no mating season. Mating occurs throughout the year. Leopardesses are sexually receptive at three-to-seven-week intervals when they are in heat/estrus for seven days. Estrus reoccurs every twenty-five to fifty-eight days until conception occurs.

Behavior during estrus is typical of the cat family. A female initiates her desire to copulate by turning around and approaching a male who's been eagerly following behind her. She rubs her cheeks on him when he stops to scent mark a tree announcing his territoriality. She crouches in front of his face announcing her willingness to mate. When he mounts her, he leaps off immediately when she whirls about snarling. During the beginning days of her estrus, her courtship behavior alternates between flirting and defensiveness. She's coquettish, teasing him with her sexual advances. Responding to her advances, he eagerly approaches her but is startled and confused by her defensive spitting, scratching, and yowling. He's further confused when she writhes on the ground at his feet inviting him to approach. He's not quite certain how to proceed when she flaunts her flanks at him inviting him to pursue her. When she is in full estrus, she finally yields to his romantic overtures. She shows her readiness by crouching with her head low, eyes narrowed, ears slightly back, rump elevated, tail raised and deflected. After patiently waiting with frequent, frustrated licking his erect penis, long pursuits and being rebuffed he cautiously mounts her. Surprised, she attempts to escape by twisting and scratching. To protect himself, he jumps off. Undaunted he tries again. At last, she yields to his advances by becoming passive and going limp. When he straddles her, instead of grasping her with his forelegs like most carnivores, he moves like a human. His pelvis moves thrusting his penis into her.

Patrick describes their mating. "They'll copulate for twenty-one seconds. Like Lions, those two Leopards will mate often at fifteen-minute intervals up to three hundred times or more. Male Lions have a lot of stamina, but Leopards beat their record of endurance. Leopards are superior to Lions in both noise and physical prowess. Leopard copulations are announced by noisy harsh growling, spitting, clawing, and teeth-gnashing. After ejaculation, the male symbolically bites his mate by baring his teeth. She responds by screaming, snarling, twisting, and striking him. Startled, he jumps back and growls at her. Then she lazily rolls over and licks her vulva clean. They will hunt and mate together for several days. After a week of frequent copulation, a female assumes the initiative by rubbing, rolling, and presenting to renew her tired mate's flagging interest. Like Lions, Leopards frequent copulation over a period of days induces ovulation. Barbs on his penis stimulate ovulation but cause her excruciating pain. It is necessary to stimulate the production of eggs so conception can occur. Exhausted, her consort leaves his mating ground to males who hear the mating racket and are alerted to the female's readiness to mate. Leopards are unlike Lions. Since Leopards are solitary, there is no pride with a reigning monarch to dethrone. Male Leopards arrive at the mating grounds and wait patiently and cleverly for their turn. Waiting on the sidelines is an excellent and wise strategy preventing an all-out fight to gain mating privileges. After mating successfully, Leopards will part company and recommence their life of solitude."

An impregnated Leopardess' gestation lasts from ninety to one hundred days. She'll seek shelter in a cave, thick undergrowth, or hollow tree. There she'll give birth. The birth weight of her cubs is only fourteen to twenty-one ounces. They are relatively small compared to an adult male weighing 143 pounds, but they will grow quickly. A Leopard litter of one to six cubs is born at two-year intervals. Because the newly born cubs are very tiny and weak, most die during the first hours after birth. Hungry and desperate for protein, she'll devour their bodies.

The surviving, helpless, blind cubs are hidden by their mother in rocky outcroppings, dense thickets, hollow trees, or caves. She constantly changes their hiding place sheltering them from predators of Hyenas, Baboons, and Jackals.

Cubs can see by their sixth to tenth day. During the first days of their existence, she warms them by holding them against her fur and grooms them clean. Although she is primarily nocturnal, she'll carry her young into the sun near their hideaway to warm them. She licks their tiny bodies to separate their fur exposing their skin to the sun's rays for Vitamin D When they are three weeks old, their mother remains close to them, straying no further than a few feet. During the first few months, she spends 55% to 66% of her time with her cubs. Most of that time, 62% is spent with them at night and 38% during the day. After spending about thirty-three hours with them, she'll leave them for up to thirty-six hours going no further than a mile from their hiding place. When they reach two months, she'll shorten her time with them. Half of that time is spent with them, about thirty-nine hours, and leaves them up to twenty-five hours. While away, she spends the time hunting, feeding on a large kill and guarding it against Hyenas, Vultures, and Jackals. When she returns to her cubs, her contact call is 'Urr-urr-urr.'

As they grow older, she gradually leaves them for longer periods and ranges about eight miles from their den. The length of time and distances traveled are dependent on finding, killing, and protecting her prey from scavengers. While she's away, her cubs don't leave their hideaway. If they wander away, they're easy prey for hungry predators.

Photo by unsplash

A Leopardess ensures that her cubs are safe by keeping them hidden until they are six weeks old. Reaching that age, they'll venture out and go on short excursions with their mother. They follow her tail with its conspicuous white tip arched over her back. Her tail is the cubs' first toy. When they stray from her, she summons them calling with loud, abrupt purrs.

Cubs are weaned as early as three months. Once they are weaned, their mother leads them to her kill and teaches them how to feed. However, they'll continue to be dependent on their mother for at least a year. She encourages them to leave her when they are eighteen to twenty months. By then they can fend for themselves having learned hunting skills from observing their mother.

Patrick posed a question that puzzled our group. "Of all the large African carnivores, the Leopard outranks the Cheetah in the predator pecking order. Those cubs will grow into powerful adults with lethal striking claws. As Princes of Stealth, they are more powerful and intimidating than Hyenas. In spite of that appearance, rangers and scientists are mystified as to why a Leopard turns tail and allows Hyenas to steal their kill and chase him up a tree. Is it because of an inferiority complex? Is it because they're loners and are unnerved by confrontations?"

"As antisocial animals, do they always run from other animals?" I ask. "Do they have enemies? Is a Leopardess as protective as a Lioness with her cubs? Like a mother Lion, does a Leopardess abandon a single cub?"

"Regarding running from other animals," responds Patrick, "sometimes Leopards are killed by Lions, Wild Dogs, Spotted Hyenas, and Crocodiles. Aging and ill Leopards are easy prey. Cubs straying from their hideout, or their protective mother are fair game for those predators. Leopards turn tail, avoiding confrontations by running away. However, a Leopardess with young cubs will take the offensive. Rather than running from a ravenous Hyena preying on her young, she'll fiercely and viciously attack him. She'll victoriously tear her smaller opponent to pieces. She will not abandon any of her young."

Wild Dogs   Photo by unsplash

We drive away allowing others to view our Leopardess and her young cubs. On the way, James spots a herd of Impalas. Their eyes reflect round, wide spots of yellow light. We compare the differences between predator's and prey's eyes allowing the fittest to survive.

Patrick surprises us when he drives into a boma (open, natural space) with a fire blazing in its pit. Near the welcoming warmth of the fire are tables with linen tablecloths, candles, and place settings. Several Land Rovers with adventurers from our camp join us. Our last meal of wild game, delicious South African cuisine and wines are served in the boma. My group toasts James and Patrick thanking them for finding and teaching us about the Big Five and Little Five.

We add that we hope to see the carnivorous Leopard's counterpart, the herbivorous Leopard Tortoise during our last game drive in the morning.

HERBIVOROUS - THE LEOPARD TORTOISE

Geochelone pardalis

After an early breakfast, our group leaves for our last game drive. We're hoping to find the grass-eating, herbivorous Leopard Tortoise. Little Five's counterpart to the Big Five's Leopard.

During our drive we pass herds of Impala, Wildebeest, and Thomson's and Grant's Gazelles. Patrick points at a Waterbuck with his 'follow me sign.' This marking resembles a toilet seat on his rear. We're told this is like the Leopard cubs following their mother's "follow me" white marking on the tip of her tail. Like tail markings, Waterbucks follow their mothers' "toilet seat" markings.

James points at a sausage tree. Lolling on one of its branches is a sleeping Leopard. He's in the classic Leopard's repose position where his body is draped on the branch with spotted legs hanging over it.

At midmorning, Patrick stops on a grassy knoll. He and James set up a table for our morning snack of grapes, fresh pieces of pineapple, croissants, papaya jam, passion fruit jelly, Jack and Cheddar cheese, hard-boiled eggs, delicious Boerewors (South African spicy beef and pork sausage), hot chocolate, tea, and coffee. The hot beverages and delicious breakfast snacks warm us during our last cold morning on South Africa's savanna.

Photo by unsplash

James wanders off. We watch him walking and looking intently at the grass. Suddenly he waves and gestures beckoning us to him. When we join him, he points at a hole and tells us that it is an abandoned Jackal hole. At its opening a beak, then a speckled head with beady, black eyes slowly appears. Its leathery head on a very short neck is followed by front legs that are paddle shaped with small nails on bird-like toes. In front of its shell is a V-shaped notch. We're told that shape allows it to withdraw its neck rapidly. Its shell or carapace is high and domed with pyramid-shaped, plate-like projections. The creature's rear legs are thick and club-like with scales and claws on their toes. We're informed that in spite of their stubby legs, the animal in front of us is capable of moving fast on its stubby feet. Its unique, attractive markings of black Leopard spots on a creamy-yellow carapace readily identify it. It's a Leopard Tortoise, the world's fourth largest tortoise. Africa supports more of these land tortoises than anywhere else in the world. Once you know what and where to find them, you'll see Tortoises crossing roads and grazing on grasslands.

Photo by Hal Brindley, travel 4 wildlife

Patrick says, "This Leopard Tortoise is humongous! It's at least twenty-eight inches in length from his neck to his tail. He must weigh close to 120 pounds. The length of his carapace probably measures around twenty-four inches. A typical adult's length measuring from head to tail is eighteen inches and weight is forty pounds. The circumference of typical adults' shells is 39 inches. Leopard Tortoises don't dig except when they make a nest. They look for abandoned, deep holes dug by Jackals, Foxes and Anteaters. Thanks to James' keen eyes locating this Jackal's former home, you're looking at the Leopard's Little Five counterpart, the Leopard Tortoise. Leopard Tortoises are cold-blooded animals. We, as humans, are warm-blooded with a constant temperature of 98.6 degrees Fahrenheit. Leopard Tortoises are most active during the morning when temperatures are comfortable for them. As you've experienced during your safari, temperatures on the savanna are cool in the morning and hot during the day, cooling again in the evening. Night temperatures are cold. As humans, we accommodate to changes in temperature with jackets and blankets when it's cold and remove them when the temperature rises. Obviously, a Leopard Tortoise, a reptile, doesn't have that luxury. As cold-blooded reptiles, their body temperatures changes with the fluctuations of their environmental temperature. Literally, their blood could boil when sun rays increase temperatures during the day. In order to survive, Leopard Tortoises adapt by being most active early in the morning and just before the sun goes down when temperatures are moderate. We're fortunate to see him as he'll return to his shelter during the hottest time of the day. To avoid the cold night temperatures, he went to sleep early last night. Those scutes or "plates" that cover his shell provide not only coloration, but also serve as insulation. They protect Leopard Tortoises against sudden changes in temperature. For further protection, Tortoises find an abandoned hole, hibernating during cold weather and estivating (going dormant) when it's hot. Watch him as he's now leaving his large shelter to spend most of this morning grazing on mixed grasses."

While Patrick is speaking to us, James goes to the table with our breakfast snacks. He returns with a cluster of grapes. James removes several grapes and places them near our Leopard Tortoise.

"Leopard Tortoises have a keen sense of smell," says Patrick. "They have no ears but make up for that lack by sensing vibrations enabling them to move around in their environment. This guy felt the vibration of James feet. Instead of leaving the area because of the vibrating ground, the Tortoise is remaining. His keen sense of smell is detecting the grapes James placed near him. Leopard Tortoises are herbivorous. They eat green grass, herbs, fallen fruit, and fungi. Occasionally, they'll chew on bones or Hyenas' feces as a source of calcium for their shells. Their source of water in an arid environment is the fruit and pads of prickly pear cactus and other succulents. Water is stored in large anal sacs that occupy most of the space in their abdominal cavities. Those spaces are a very important adaptation enabling them to survive in a dry environment."

Our Leopard Tortoise finds the grapes. We watch him peck at the grapes with his beak. Patrick comments that Turtles and Tortoises do not have teeth. They bite and rip into food with their hard, sharp, beak-like mouths.

"Patrick, I have a friend who has two large pet Tortoises housed in a huge terrarium. She says she'd rather have Tortoises and not Turtles. What's the difference between the two?"

Turtles   Photo by Isabel Kronemberger, unsplash

Patrick answers, "Turtles and Tortoises are relatives. They both belong to the taxonomic order, *Chelonia*, Greek for Tortoise. Leopard Tortoises are classified as *Geo*, Greek meaning earth or land and *Chelone* meaning Tortoise. Their species or specific name is *padalis* from Latin meaning leopard, referring to the leopard-like spots that you see on his shell. From its classification, *Geo*, he is a land-dwelling reptile. Notice his shell. It's domed and not flat. The shape of Tortoises' shells depends on their species and habitat. Dry land-dwelling Tortoises have high-domed shells, which help protect them from the jaws of predators. A rounded dome allows a Tortoise to quickly withdraw his legs and head for protection. Both Turtles and Tortoises have 'scutes' or bony scales or plates on their shells. Since they are land dwellers, they are not hydrodynamic. Their bodies are stumper and not shaped for living in water. Their round body is carried on stubby, strong legs. Turtles have a streamlined body with a flat shell allowing them to glide through water. Water dwellers have flippers for swimming, the non-aquatic *Chelones* don't. Furthermore, Turtles can hold their breath while swimming under water. Tortoises living in arid regions are capable, as I mentioned earlier, of storing their water. Their feet are adapted for walking on sandy, grassy ground. Biologically speaking, a Tortoise is a kind of a Turtle, but not all Turtles are Tortoises! To distinguish between the two, land dwellers are referred to as Tortoises and aquatic ones are called Turtles. Turtles live in freshwater, the ocean, brackish ponds or underwater. They even mate and lay their eggs underwater. Some will venture to dry land to lay eggs. When those eggs hatch, the baby turtles hurry straight into water. Turtles, such as Sea Turtles, migrate great distances. Tortoises don't, they remain within their home range. Unlike Turtles, they live entirely above water. The only contact they have with water is when they wade into it to bathe or to quench their thirst. In fact, they could drown in deep water or be swept away by strong currents. Their feet, unlike flippers on Turtles, are hard, scaly, and nubby on strong, short legs enabling them to crawl across sharp rocks and sand. Tortoises are larger than their cousins. Also, the land dwellers have a pointy claw and mouth or beak. Tortoises are herbivorous, plant eaters. Turtles are omnivorous, eating plants, insects, and fish. Another member of this order, Terrapins, falls between Tortoises and Turtles. They live in both water and on land. Most live-in swampy water, in ponds, lakes and rivers. Scientists consider them to be more closely related to Turtles than to Tortoises. Some Terrapins are born in water and leave it for dry land."

Patrick continues his dialogue about the large, attractively marked Leopard Tortoise in front of us. Like his Big Five counterpart, the Leopard, Leopard Tortoises are beautiful and solitary animals. He states that these loners are the most widely distributed Tortoise in Southern Africa. These Tortoises are one of the most successful animals on the savanna. They are the fourth largest species of Tortoise in the world. The three preceding them are the Sulcata, Galapagos, and Seychelles Giant Tortoise.

James points at another Leopard Tortoise ambling towards our feeding one. Patrick looks at it, commenting, "Moving towards us is a female. She may have smelled the grapes or saw him feeding on them. Leopard Tortoises have a well-developed sense of smell and taste. Their eyesight is excellent. She's a female because she's smaller but broader than him."

One of us inquires, "Besides size, what else distinguishes a female from a male? Can you identify the age of these Tortoises?"

Patrick responds with, "Fortunately the two are near each other. Look at their tails. The male has a longer and thicker tail."

As soon as Patrick picks up the male by his shell, we are startled by the Tortoise's response. He has a bowel movement and urinates. Fortunately, Patrick's arm is extended away, clasping the Tortoise's shell in the middle. Chuckling, Patrick comments that he was prepared for the Tortoise's defensive response. After defecating and urinating, the threatened creature draws his head straight back into his shell and pulls his forelegs in front of his sheltered head. Only his front legs are exposed. Patrick points at the exposed legs saying that they are covered with enlarged scales for protection.

Patrick turns the male Tortoise over. He says, "Besides size and length of tails, you can tell that this is a male because the angle of the scutes (plates) near his tail is straighter than the female's sharper angle. This is his cloacal opening. It leads to his cloaca which is a common chamber for all amphibians', reptiles', and birds' feces, urine, and sex organs. A male Leopard Tortoise's cloacal opening is closer to his tail. A female's opening is further from the tail to accommodate the passage of eggs. Look between the cloaca and his tail's root. That's where his penis is located. Also, a male has a cupped plastron or belly. That cupped belly is placed over a female's domed shell while mating."

Returning the male back to the ground, Patrick exposes the female's belly. "Notice that her belly is flat. When he mounts her, she is flattened against the ground. Also, as I mentioned, look at the angle of her plates near her tail. The angle of her plates is sharper. These adults are not as brightly marked like younger Tortoises. The background of older Tortoise shells is a varied shade of yellow with small brown spots. Younger Tortoises' spots are dark brown or black and larger."

Patrick says, "Tortoises have a long life, up to seventy-five years in the wild. Because of their longevity, they seldom mature until they are between twelve and fifteen years old. Although Tortoises are smaller than their warm-blooded relatives, the males are surprisingly well-endowed. A male's penis is anatomically and physiologically like that of mammals. Like mammals, his reproductive appendage is a single, erectile organ. Unlike the Red-billed Buffalo Weaver's false phallus, a male Tortoise has many blood vessels and an expandable corpus spongiosum or body of spongy tissue. As his phallus inflates, its length increases by 50%, its width 75% and length 10%. An erect penis is about half the size of his body's length. So, for this twenty-eight-inch male, it's approximately fourteen inches. When it's not erected, his penis is doubled up on itself inside his cloaca. When excited, his penis un-doubles and protrudes. Once I observed a male Tortoise bathing and drinking. He submerged the front half of his body and rose on his back leg. I watched as he dropped his large, dark-purple penis in the water and retracted it back into his cloaca. He repeated his odd behavior several times. I've been told that Tortoise's phallus is always dark-grey, purple, or blackish. The head of his sexual organ is expanded and tipped with a sharp spine that allows him to maintain his hold of a female's cloaca while mating."

We listen to Patrick as he continues telling us of the Leopard Tortoises' courtship and mating. There is no breeding season for Leopard Tortoises. However, their peak breeding period is during the rainy season. Competing over a female, males will butt each other until one is overturned by the victor. A male courts a female by ramming and mounting her. His courtship is characterized by lengthy pursuits and aggressive encounters. Attempting to attract her attention, he nips her feet and strikes her with his heavy shell. Succeeding in climbing on top of her, he attempts to mate. Not interested in his efforts, she dashes for safety towards and into bushes. Her suitor clings determinedly and desperately on top of her shell. She fails to shake off her clinging suitor. Triumphantly, he seizes his opportunity to mate. Un-doubled from his cloaca, he repeatedly inserts his erect phallus into and out of her cloaca. Throughout his mating, he vocalizes his endeavors with grunts. Climaxing, he ejaculates implanting her with his sperm. Afterwards, he dismounts and returns to his solitary life.

Photo by Hal Brindley, travel 4 wildlife

She gestates for a few weeks. Nesting occurs between May and October. When ready to lay her leathery, round, white fertilized eggs, she softens the soil with her urine. Using her hind legs, she digs a hole about a foot across and twelve inches deep. About five to thirty eggs are deposited in the hole. Using her shell, she taps on the soil by lifting and dropping it and packing it over her nesting cavity. Repeating her mating with other males, she buries a brood of eggs about once a month. Leopard Tortoises have the longest egg incubation period of a year. Hatchlings break their shells with their eye teeth. They wait several weeks for rain to soften the surrounding soil allowing them to dig their way out of their nest. Hatchlings are yellow with one to two black spots on each of their shells' plates. They are entirely on their own. As soon as they surface, they go immediately into hiding and feeding on a variety of plants. Because of the high-water content of succulents, hatchlings prefer succulents. When they are about three to five years, they are large enough to go into the open and escape from their predators. Young are easy prey for Monitor Lizards, Storks, Crows, small mammals, and the crushing jaws of Lions and Hyenas.

Patrick continues his dialogue. "Few animals attempt to prey on adult Leopard Tortoises. Tortoises may not be quick but their main form of defense, pulling their entire body inside an impregnable fortress of a shell is almost fool proof. Also, you saw their other defensive, defecating weapon that startles predators such as man when they attempt to move them. If you see a Leopard Tortoise crossing a road, don't hesitate to pick him up and carry him to safety. Inattentive drivers kill them each year. If you do pick one up, look for the ticks that cling to the edges of the plates. They're perfectly camouflaged, matching the Leopard's print."

Unfortunately, we learn that like all the animals we've seen, these beautiful reptiles could be threatened. The multiple eggs enable their species to survive. However, there is no overpopulation of Leopard Tortoises because the balance of nature is maintained by predators. Incubating eggs and/or embryos are found by them and devoured. Once again, man is this Tortoise's worse enemy. Leopard Tortoises and its eggs are hunted for food. People search for nesting eggs and remove the yolk and egg white or the developing embryo from the shell. Emptied shells are cleaned to be used as containers or as sound boxes for musical instruments. Leopard Tortoises are not considered seriously threatened because they are widespread throughout South Africa. However, they are under increasing pressure from habitat loss due to man's slashing and burning of wood and grass lands, global warming changing seasonal patterns, and being heavily exploited by the pet trade. An unsuspecting pet owner doesn't realize that he or she will be outlived by their pet Tortoise. The average life span of captive Tortoises is between eighty and one hundred years."

We've succeeded in finding 90% of the animals we sought throughout our safari. Thanks to Patrick and James, we saw all the Big Five: The Elephant, Cape Buffalo, Rhino, Lion, and Leopard, and four of the Little Five: Red-billed Buffalo Weaver, Rhinoceros Beetle, Ant Lion, and the Leopard Tortoise. The Elephant Shrew continued to elude us throughout our game drives and walking safari. We're comforted by the thought that with the Shrew's exception, we accomplished our goal of finding and learning about each animal's intriguing behavior.

Africa's wildlife captivated my group of adventurers. Like most tourists who've experienced the thrill of being on safari, they've been infected by an incurable condition of "Africanitis," wanting to return to Eastern and Southern Africa for more game drives. Each of us is determined to return to the exciting continent of Africa to discover more about its animal and plant life.

The Dark Continent   Photo by Patrick Karst

CHAPTER 11

SAFARI!

Nzuri sana

Big Five Tours and Expeditions introduced me to my first safari departing on August 1, 1985, on Virgin Atlantic from Los Angeles via Heathrow, London, to Nairobi, Kenya. Our group was met and greeted with "Jambo" (Swahili—hello) by our guide/driver, Wilson. We left Kenyatta International Airport for our luxurious, all-suite hotel, built in 1984, the Nairobi Safari Club. Centrally located, it was perfect for browsing local sights and shopping.

The Ark   Photo by unsplash

Our safari life began in a Land Rover driving toward the highlands to Aberdare National Park. Box, our spotter, was riding tandem on the Rover's front fender. After a sumptuous lunch at Aberdare Country Club, we packed an overnight bag and headed to the Aberdare Mountains for an overnight at the Ark. The rustic lodge has viewing balconies providing game viewing of animals attracted to the waterhole and salt lick, flood lit at night. Kibwe, the night watchman buzzed our rooms that night to inform us of animals sighted at the waterhole. Having gone to bed fully clothed, we lost no time in racing to the balconies with our cameras. Our photo op was of a lioness and her cubs thirstily lapping water. Later, I saw Kibwe. I greeted him in Swahili saying, "Asante Sana" (thank you), adding, "Nzuri Sana (very good)!

After breakfast, we're off to the heart of Kenya's "Big Game" country and Ol Pejeta's Sweetwater Tented Camp. During my first night at the camp, a laughing hyena lulled me to sleep. The 110,000-acre private ranch is rich with different animals wandering its plains, low hills, and forest. We spotted reticulated giraffe, Cape Buffalo, zebra, and oryx. We visited endangered chimpanzees in their sanctuary, the only place they may be seen in Kenya. During the night game drive, an irate, rumbling bull elephant chased us while Wilson calmly backed away. He explained that Mr. Elephant was in musth (sexually aroused).

After two nights at Sweetwater, we headed for the famous Mt. Kenya Safari Club founded by the late movie star, Bill Holden, and his friends in 1959. The luxurious hotel is at Mt. Kenya's foot. There we relaxed among the international jet set of the rich and famous. We shopped, swam in the pool, some went horseback riding or golfing. We enjoyed bird watching peacocks, semi-tamed sacred ibises, marabou stocks, Egyptian geese, and colorful, small, exotic birds flitting hungrily among our breakfast and lunch tables. The highlight of the day was the Animal Orphanage, housing endangered mountain bongo, cheetahs, blue monkeys, Sykes monkeys, and rescued wild animals injured by poachers.

Saying "Asante Sana" and "Kwaheri" (good-bye) to the staff, we drove northward to Samburu National Reserve. Two nights camping on the reserve were insufficient! Samburu is a gem—my favorite! We spotted the fascinating Gerenuk, one of Samburu special five. The others are: Beisa oryx, Grevy's zebra, Reticulated giraffe, and Somali ostrich. Samburu is a birder's mecca! More than 390 species have been recorded on the reserve. Notables are: Vulturine guinea fowl, Somali bee eater, Golden-breasted starling, White-bellied bustard, and Black-capped social weaver.

Traveling south, we arrived at Lake Nakuru National Park. The lake boasts the most spectacular of all Africa's bird sights. Enormous flocks of flaming pink flamingos glide above crystal blue waters.

After breakfast in our Lake Nakuru Lodge, we drove to the famous Masai Mara Game Reserve.

We were in time for the migration which occurs during the dry months of July to October. It's the greatest natural show on earth! We watched thousands of wildebeests, zebras, and gazelles scrambling down muddy banks, unlucky ones seized by hungry, large Nile crocodiles in the Mara River before they could escape to the opposite shore toward Tanzania.

Africa's wildlife is spectacular and unforgettable! After an exciting and educational safari, I departed from Nairobi with many fond memories and incurable Africanitis.

Since 1985, I've been on innumerable safaris throughout East and South Africa seeing and hearing the migration in Kenya and Tanzania, viewing giraffes peeking over bushes on an island from a Land Rover in Botswana's Okavango Delta, bird watching in Zimbabwe, trekking for gorillas in Uganda, viewing herds of elephants in Namibia, and searching for the Big and Little Five in South Africa.

While packing for a safari, consider practicality, comfort, and light. I attach a Magellan's retriever tag with my itinerary to my luggage and include an itinerary in an outside pocket. My luggage and backpack are light, soft-sided, and squashable. Internal flights and flights to lodges are restricted to twelve to fifteen kilograms. Luggage on the smaller aircrafts is squished and squeezed to accommodate the small aircraft's compartment. My clothes are light, practical, and blended with the environment. I have a travel jacket with zip off sleeves and a vest with innumerable pockets, useful for my iPhone, ear plugs, face mask, eye mask, neck pillow, snacks, Colgate on-the-go toothbrush, malaria pills, saline nose spray, and medications. All items I need in case the airline misplaces my luggage are packed in my backpack: toothbrush, toothpaste, hairbrush, camera, memory cards, adapter, chargers, extension cord, iPad and charger, binoculars, nightgown, one set of underwear, a pair of zoris, and a pair of socks. My passport holder contains my passport, International Certificate of Vaccination, $100 USD in $10, $5, $1 denominations for tips and sundries, travel documents, and $100 in my destination's currency.

Before my cab driver, Alex Hemans (310 908-7455) arrives, I swallow Airborne Vitamin C. I'll follow this regime until the third day at the camp and when I return through three days in my home. Arriving at the airport, I check in and go through TSA's inspection. Before leaving TSA, I ascertain that my passport is safely in my vest. Before boarding the aircraft, next, I fill my collapsible water bottle. When my plane leaves the tarmac, I chew and swallow a No Jet Lag (homeopathic remedy), and will continue doing so, (per its directions) until we arrive in Africa. No Jet Lag will successfully help in adjusting my biological clock. I resist the temptation to nap. My circadian rhythm is adjusted by going to bed no earlier than 9:00 p.m. I've traveled to 180 countries and never suffered from jet lag.

My Tasco binoculars and travel items are from Rei, Nikon Coolpix from Costco, my jacket and vest from Magellan, travel pants (removable legs) and shirts (removable sleeves) from Travel Smith. The boots are from Big 5 Sporting Goods.

Binoculars:

Tasco 7X35 with caps and travel bag.
A fellow passenger had a 50x10 DPS with caps and travel bag.
Guides use Nikon 10x42 Prostaff.
Spotters do not need binoculars.

Photography:

Nikon Coolpix 8700, digital, 35-280 mm (zoom up to 4x).
Lens cleaner.

Memory cards.

Spare batteries.

Battery charger, adapter.

Electrical power adapter, South Africa.

Electrical plug South Africa, three prongs, round, large.

Extension electrical cord.

South Africa plug type: D&M.

Several in my group successfully used camera phones (some lodges ban camera phones on game drives because their geolocation has been used by poachers).

Most lodges have a place where you may recharge your batteries, iPhone, and iPad. Not all lodges have the availability in their tents.

Necessities:

Airborne Vitamin C, Day and Night.

Alarm Clock.

Body lotion.

Book—there'll be a lot of free time when you're at the camp. Refer to Reference for ideas as to which books you have room to pack in your luggage. Books to read between game drives and meals. If the camp has Wi-Fi, I read books from my iPad.

Bungee clothesline. (I hand wash my underwear and clothes when the lodges do not have laundry service. The upscale ones offer free laundry service.)

Colgate Wisp Max Free: brush-on-the-go.

Collapsible water bottle. Cool pix: dental floss and toothpick.

Contact lenses with wetting and soaking solutions.

Copies of passport, passport photos, credit card, emergency contacts.

Deodorant (fragrant less).

Digital luggage hand scale.

Duct and Scotch Tape.

Dust mask.

Ear plugs.

Eye drops.

Facial cleanser.

Facial moisturizer.

First aid kit: Neosporin, band aids, bandage, tape.

Flashlight, Maglite.

Flat rubber/silicon sink cover for hand laundry.

Glasses.

Hand wipes.

Hand sanitizer.

iPad and charger.

iPhone and charger.

Imodium/anti-diarrhea medications.

Insect repellant with Deet and/or safari clothes with embedded Deet.

Ivory soap for hand laundry.

Kleenex.

Lens tissues.

Pepto Bismol pills (I take two before each meal).

Prescribed medications.

Probulin-probiotics.

Malaria Pills.

No Jet Lag.

Safety pins.

Saline Nasal Spray-for flights.

Scarf.

Snacks.

Sunglasses.

Sunscreen (I recommend titanium oxide and zinc oxide. Avoid carcinogenic ingredients: parabpon, and sodium laureth sulfate. (NO fragrances while on safari!)

Recommended by scientists: for the body – The Organic Pharmacy Cellular Protection.

Toilet paper with cardboard (insert removed).

Toothbrush.

Toothpaste.

U.S. Embassy Address.

Walking sticks (folding).

Washcloth.

Ziplock bags, all sizes, three to five each, rolled and rubber banded.

Most game lodges provide bath soaps and shampoo; just in case they do not, I pack a small bottle of shampoo, conditioner, and bath soap.

NO NOS:

Bright colors.

Cologne/perfume.

Cosmetics (takes up space).

Dress.

Dressy shoes.

Jewelry.

Clothing: Neutral-colored, earth tones—tans, greens, grays, brown. Mine are khaki colored.

I've learned to select my safari clothing for comfort lightness, neutral color, has Deet embedded in it, and offers protection from the sun with an SPF rating of 50+. So I will not have to wash every night and not smell the next day, I look for clothing that is made of anti-microbial or anti-bacterial fabric. Whenever I travel, I layer my clothing. I wear compression stockings for the twenty hours from Los Angeles via the East coast to Johannesburg. Meeting the luggage weight restrictions, I lighten the weight by wearing my boots and layer my heaviest clothing on the flight.

These are my clothing items:

One bathing suit with light robe.

Two blouses—zip- off collar and sleeves.

Five each of bras and panties.

One hat, broad brim, khaki. Game lodges or safari companies may provide bush hats.

One Jacket, light weight, windbreaker (for night drives) or heavier if safari is during the winter. Blankets are provided during night drives. I have a jacket and a vest with numerous pockets and zip off sleeves. Using either one, I leave my day pack at home.

One light nightgown.

Two pants, zip off into shorts.

One shower cap.

One pair of light, hiking boots.

One pair sneaker.

Five of wicking socks with Deet.

One pair of zoris. For shower and swimming pool.

I wear the following when I'm on safaris during Africa's winter:

Gloves.

Scarf.

Woolen socks.

Warm Hat.

Whenever I travel, I pack clothes that I no longer want. I leave them behind at my destinations providing space to pack my purchases of African masks, animal motif jewelry and T-shirts.

Dressing in khaki and comfortable boots while on safari is not only practical but has its dividends. After a successful game drive, we stopped near a waterhole for our customary sundowner.

I asked for and received permission to leave the Land Rover for the bush while Wilson and Box organized our drinks and snacks. Locating a large bush camouflaging me from my group, I provided moisture to the parched earth. The dirty Kleenex was placed in a Ziplock bag. Leaving the safety of the bush, I heard hysterical, frantic yelling from the group. I noticed and wondered why Wilson and Box were carrying rifles.

"DOROTHY!"

"HURRY!"

"RUN!"

Unaware of the cause of their shouts, afraid of stumbling, I continued my snail's pace. Upon reaching the group, I was grabbed and lifted into the vehicle and stumbled onto my seat. When I left the bush's safety, a nearby leopard saw and stalked me. While surrounded by the bush, my clothes blended with its branches.

Fortunately, I did not run! I remembered Wilson instructing us during our walks "to become trees" and "never run when an animal approaches." My true-life adventure nearly ended as prey in Ms. Leopard's mouth and food for her kitties.!

TIPPING: Tour operators usually include this advice in their documents. If not:

Tips can be paid in US dollars or local currency:

Driver/guide - US$10 and upward per day. Private safari guide - US$25 and upward per day. Camp staff - $10 to $20 per day, as a pooled tip to be shared among the housekeepers, waiters, bartender, etc.

Enjoy an unforgettable and thrilling safari, hearing the roar of mating lions, falling asleep, lulled by the laughter of hyenas, observing frolicking baby elephants, watching Buffalo Weavers flit in and outbuilding their nest, or searching for the elusive leopard. Without a doubt, you'll leave our world's second largest continent with fond memories of a true-life adventure, incredible photos, and Africanitis.

Photo by Dorothy Van Horn

REFERENCES

African Wildlife Foundation, www.awf.org/blog/going-tuskless

Ballard, S. (2000). *Footprint: South Africa, Handbook 2000.* Footprint Handbooks.

Caruthers, V. (1997), T*he Wildlife of Southern Africa.* Southern Book Publication.

Estes, R. D. (1992). *The Behavior Guide to African Mammals.* The University of California Press.

Estes, R. D. (1993). *The Safari Companion.* Chelsea Green Publishing Company.

Fitzpatrick, M., Blond, B. Pitcher, G., Richmond, S., & Warren, M. (2015). *South Africa, Lesotho & Swaziland.* Lonely Planet

Frandsen, R. (1992). *Southern African Mammals-a field guide).* Frandsen Publishers.

MacDonald, J. (10/08/20). South Africa Guide: Planning Your Trip from https://www.tripsavvy.com/south-africa-travel-guide-1454536. Tripsavvy.com

Nolting, M. W. (1994). *Africa's Top Wildlife Countries.* Global Travel Publishers, INC.

Rhinoceros-Daggers and Drugs-Young People's Trust for the Environment

shutterstock.com

unsplash.com

www.deseret.com